BECAUSE OUR FATHERS LIED

A Memoir of Truth and Family,

from Vietnam to Today

Craig McNamara

Little, Brown and Company

New York   Boston   London

Little, Brown and Company
Hachette Book Group
1290 Avenue of the Americas, New York, NY 10104
littlebrown.com

First Edition: May 2022

Little, Brown and Company is a division of Hachette Book Group, Inc. The Little, Brown name and logo are trademarks of Hachette Book Group, Inc.

The publisher is not responsible for websites (or their content) that are not owned by the publisher.

The Hachette Speakers Bureau provides a wide range of authors for speaking events. To find out more, go to hachettespeakersbureau.com or call (866) 376-6591.

Unless otherwise indicated, all photographs are from the author's collection.

ISBN 9780316282239
LCCN 2021944446

Printing 1, 2022

LSC-C

Printed in the United States of America

To Margaret McKinstry Craig.
She gave me her maiden name, her Pacific-blue
eyes, and her love of nature. It is her love that has
guided my life's journey.

CONTENTS

CONTENTS

PROLOGUE

If any question why we died
Tell them, because our fathers lied
Rudyard Kipling

Just tell me the truth. Seems simple enough. Yet for all of my life, I struggled to arrive at the truth with my father. He never told me that he knew the Vietnam War wasn't winnable. But he did know, and he never admitted it to me. More than a decade after his death, I still wonder why he was no more honest with me than he was with the American public.

When I was a kid, my parents were infallible, like two gods. My life revolved around my mother and father: the peace of our family, the security of my school, friends, and home. We lived in Washington, DC, among the rest of America's sometime deities, those who in 1964 still remained from Camelot.

I remember the familiar arched hallway of our three-story house. We had huge double doors at the entrance. Our hall-way mirror reflected my mom's stairway planter, as lush as an indoor greenhouse. Coming home from school each day, I'd search for a snack in the faded yellow kitchen. I never had to wait long for my mother's embrace. My dog Michael, a golden retriever, was always present. In the evenings and on the weekends, my parents and I would walk beneath the elms and flowering dogwoods of Rock Creek Park. These were brisk walks. Nothing slowed my dad down, neither the scent of the azaleas nor the ephemeral sense that we were at peace.

On Sunday mornings, two or three newspapers arrived at our front door. I would retrieve them and bring them into the kitchen. Dad would unfold the newspapers on the dining room table and read them from cover to cover, with a furrowed brow and clenched jaw and with his blue china coffee cup poised in his left hand. I could hear Mom scrambling eggs with her wire whisk, roasting bacon, and toasting Dad's favorite whole wheat Thomas' English Muffins. My role was to sit quietly at the table.

I don't think it was mere silence that my father required at breakfast. Rather, it was a moment of peace in what must have been days of striving, a hurried and demanding life. Invariably on those quiet Sunday mornings, the kitchen phone would ring. My dad would answer, and after clearing his throat with a short cough, the first words out of his mouth would be "Yes, Mr. President."

Pause.

"Well, Marg was planning on making cheeseburgers for Craigie and me, and maybe some tennis in the afternoon."

Another pause. I couldn't hear what President Johnson was saying on the other end of the line, but I could hear his voice in my head. That familiar drawl was not yet threatening. A smile formed on my lips.

"Oh, yes, Mr. President. We'll be there."

Shortly after the call, we all got into the blue Ford Galaxy with DC license plates (#3) and drove through the empty avenues of Washington to the White House. There wasn't much traffic in those days, and the drive wasn't long. This trip happened several times, but I never got used to it.

The guard at the entry gate leading into the Rose Garden raised the iron post as we arrived. We drove up to the White House, where the President was waiting to greet us. With his sweet Texan demeanor, Lyndon Johnson leaned over to my mom, gave her a big kiss, and said, "Margy, it's so nice to have you and Bob come by. Bring that boy of yours up to our family dining room, as I know he must be starving."

In the dining room, President Johnson sat at one end of a deeply polished mahogany table, with Lady Bird at the other end. The ceilings were high, the walls painted with murals of colonial scenes. The room was both grand and intimate—warm but also echoing and exposed. Dad was seated to the President's left, Mom to his right. To this day, I can't remember where I sat. Perhaps these experiences were too overwhelming for me to form memories. I do remember that the President was always gracious and generous.

After lunch, the President suggested that we take a dip in the indoor pool. What he really meant was that I was to take a dip while he and my father discussed the escalating war. I changed into my suit and jumped in. I kept my head above the surface, treading water in the deep end and thinking all the time about how a young American man ought to look, what face he should make. Above me, the ceiling was all blue skies and puffy clouds—painted on, peace distilled beneath the roof. From the far end of the pool, I could see the President and his loyal secretary of defense hunched over a coffee table stacked high with briefing papers. Now and then a few words reached me, the tone of a man's voice above the lapping water, but I didn't know what they were saying.

I can imagine it was fraught. The President had called his closest adviser on a Sunday morning to support him in what must have been a lonely and torturous time in the White House. The war was ramping up. What were they planning? What disastrous paths were they debating as their wives chatted comfortably nearby?

Floating in the White House pool, I had a sense that I was included in something important. I always hoped for a family day on the weekends, always wanted to go on a walk with my mom and dad, maybe play tennis, but a trip to the White House was incredibly exciting. These were strange and magical experiences for a thirteen-year-old kid. With my two older sisters already off to college and adult life, it was just me and my parents. Visiting the White House, I felt special.

The day after our lunch and swim, I sent the President and Mrs. Johnson a handwritten thank-you note. Just a few days later, I received a letter back from President Johnson. For a man about to drag a nation into war, he was quite prompt in his replies. The final line of his letter read, "You were cheerful to be around."

That pretty well sums up how I thought I could and should support my father in those days. I swam near him, never went too far from his waters, and put on the right face. All thoughts of the war hovered somewhere between my head and the ceiling. I was unaware of what was coming.

THE WHITE HOUSE
WASHINGTON

January 20, 1964

My dear Craig:

You couldn't have pleased me more than send
me such a thoughtful note.

I can see your parents have instilled in you the
courtesies and kindness that are as worthy as
any trait I know.

Mrs. Johnson and I enjoyed having you with us.
You were cheerful to be around.

Sincerely,

Mr. Craig McNamara
2412 Tracy Place, N. W.
Washington 8, D. C.

After our White House lunch, President Johnson responded to my thank-you note.
My father traveled to Vietnam two months later.

PART 1

1.

Window into Blindness, the Abyss

One evening, when I was fifteen years old, I called my father from boarding school. The long hallway separating my dorm from the dining hall had a wooden phone booth. I closed myself inside and looked through the glass as I waited to speak with Dad. On the oak-paneled walls of the hallway, elaborately carved wooden plaques depicted winged owls, pelicans, rowboats, and Latin mottoes. These plaques were mementoes of past graduating classes, representing young men who came before me. They stared down, reminders of what I was supposed to be. Farther down the corridor, under the massive ceiling with its old wooden rafters, four hundred students scarfed down dinner, unaware that their time was coming. We were all destined to carve a plaque, yet the outcomes of our lives after school seemed so uncertain.

St. Paul's School is tucked into the woods outside Concord, New Hampshire. The all-male institution was a pretty isolated place back then. Separated from the nearby town by the acreage of its bucolic campus, set comfortably apart from the churning seas of '60s culture, Millville (as we called it) was an island paradise—with everything we needed to eat and do and think readily at hand. It was also an incubator for rare and strange diseases of the heart and mind. You didn't get in touch with your parents unless you needed to be rescued.

Dad answered the phone with his usual chipper tone. "Looking forward to skiing with you over vacation, Craigie."

We talked for a minute, mostly about my upcoming games. I played football, hockey, and lacrosse—the model athlete. But on this night, for once, sports were far from my mind. It was the winter of 1966, and my friend Rick King, president of the New Left Club, was organizing a teach-in against the war. At length, I made my request.

"Dad, if you have any information or leaflets that support your position on the war, will you send them to me?"

Even as the words came out, I expected that he would file away my question and do nothing. For a moment, he was quiet.

"Sure, Craigie. I'll have my secretary get on it."

I remember his voice fading off. I'm not sure how we ended the conversation. I only remember an increasing distance between us, like watching a boat sail away from shore, even though I was looking at a quiet hallway through smudged glass. There was silence on the line.

When I remember that evening, I picture Dad holding the phone to his ear, and I wonder what he was thinking during that silence. Was he envisioning his most recent trip to Saigon, punctuated by talk of body counts and napalm bombings? Was he wondering how to explain it all to his only son? Or was he holding his breath, waiting for the moment to pass?

After I hung up, I wandered into the dining hall, got a plate, and sat down among boys whose fathers worked on Wall Street, owned publishing houses, or served in government and businesses across America. Although I was another kid with a powerful father, I felt distant from my peers in that moment. Over the next few days, I checked my school mailbox and asked the postmaster whether a large package of printed material had arrived for me.

I don't have very vivid memories about the teach-in itself. I remember that it was in a science classroom, filled to capacity. I was seated to the right of the speaker, Jonathan Mirsky, who was a scholar from Dartmouth. He showed us some maps of Southeast Asia. He indicated places on the maps with a long pointer, much like my father did in black-and-white newsreel images. I wasn't focused on what we were learning. For me, the meeting was more about feelings of dread, as Mirsky taught us why the war was both morally wrong and unwinnable.

It was a little dark in the room that night. I do remember that.

Rick King was one of my best friends. Representing the student perspective, he engaged in conversation with Mirsky. I still thought of Rick as my fellow defensive back, not a political activist. Taking turns returning kick-offs and punts, occasionally intercepting a pass and scoring a touchdown, he and I supported each other. On the field we were tough, speaking as we thought men should, grunting and groveling in the dirt and turf. I wasn't aware that Rick had this extra concern for humanity.

Calling Dad before the teach-in had been an attempt to learn from a primary source. I wasn't asking him to justify the war, but I wanted his perspective. *Tell me the truth, Dad—why are we there?* Yet the thing I remember most from our conversation is talking about football. As with many things in my life touching my father, what I don't remember, the absence, looms largest. It's a shadow in my mind, and my eyes are trained on the flat earth, not on the standing figure that casts it. I gave him a chance to be a part of that event, to present his own story and his own version of history, his work, but the leaflets never arrived.

Before I entered St. Paul's School, in tenth grade, I enjoyed four and a half years at Sidwell Friends School in Washington. My sister Kathleen drove me every day in our family's blue Ford Galaxy. Up Massachusetts Avenue, right at the light onto 34th Street, left onto Quebec, then into the parking lot. Sometimes we took Upton Street and passed what we were told was a home for mentally ill patients.

As a Quaker school, Sidwell valued peace and silence. The school hosted weekly Quaker meetings and lessons in compassion. Although my parents attended Presbyterian church services, to this day the Quaker faith is the only organized religion that has ever made sense to me.

At the end of eighth grade, one of my good friends at Sidwell disappeared. He came from a long lineage of St. Paul's graduates—what they call legacy kids—and he was destined to follow suit. The next summer, when he returned to Washington, he made some very convincing arguments for me to join him at boarding school. That shining campus on a hill in New England reportedly offered great sports, black ice on the ponds in the winter to skate for miles, amazing friends, and dances on weekends where you could make out with the most beautiful girls—many freedoms away from home, tradition, and family.

It was not my parents who pushed me toward St. Paul's. Looking back on that summer, I question my decision to apply and attend. Was I really motivated by my friend's stories, that prep school mythology? The year was 1964, and it was a few months after the Tonkin Gulf incident. I had zero awareness of that event, but I wonder if I had an extra sense, a foreboding that the Vietnam War was going to emotionally consume my family. Boarding school might have appeared as a way to escape. Whatever the temptation was, I was tempted. I gave in.

Upon arriving at St. Paul's, I was placed in Conover, the dorm with the motto "Where the Elite Meet." Rick King's room was just down the hall from mine. My Old Boy—an assigned big brother—was Garry Trudeau, the cartoonist who would go on to create *Doonesbury*.

The school had the sort of initiation rituals you would expect. Part of the process was receiving your nickname. I was quickly nicknamed "Missile McNamara" for my prowess as a football player. The name didn't feel like a negative comment about my father; it seemed like a compliment, with just a hint of irony. Certainly Dad's stature as head of the Defense Department conferred a degree of prestige by association. In the culture of that place, this could be the case even for those who were against the war.

I had a recollection that one of Garry's early cartoons in the school newspaper depicted me as a ballistic missile charging up the field. Garry doubts this. In conversation with me, remembering our school days, he insists that he would never have drawn such a cartoon, having been acutely aware of the ways in which nicknames were used to label and belittle underclassmen. Either I'm imagining a past that didn't exist, or another artist drew the cartoon.

Garry was one of those evolved young souls who doubted the school's traditions, finding an outlet through his artistic talents, thus surviving the whole experience. There were also scores of boys who drove hard and unquestioningly to succeed within the traditions. Everything was a competition. Our grades were displayed on the walls of the corridor leading to the dining hall. Anticipation built after exams, until some watchful boy would announce, "They just posted." I remember rushing into the hall with four hundred of my classmates, shoulder to shoulder and locked in the crowd, coming to the lists. The course titles—Latin 1, Algebra, Physics 2—were printed at the top of each page. The first time I read that list from top to bottom, I felt what became a recurring dread. I knew where I was going to be, and I just hoped that I wouldn't be there. There it was. Ninety-eight names of Fourth Formers, sophomores, all above mine. I was the son of a bitch with the worst grade. I remember being aware of other boys looking over my shoulder, surely reading my name at the bottom.

The downsides of boarding school soon outnumbered the things I liked. Yes, there were intriguing dances. But St. Paul's was an all-boys school, and I missed being around girls every day. The skating was great, but only because the campus was located in the remote woods of New Hampshire, with long winters that felt lonely and depressing. And while being away from my parents had felt liberating at first, now I was finding out that the school's adults—the rector and masters—were much more oppressive than Mom and Dad. I'd been attracted to the great privileges of that environment. After the first year, I fully understood that they came with a price.

The most difficult part was the academic rigor. I couldn't keep up. It was pretty damn discouraging to get poor grades while being the son of someone who was considered a Whiz Kid and one of the sharpest minds of his generation. After I failed most of my exams in the tenth grade, the rector, Matthew Warren, suggested to my parents that I be sent to Massachusetts General Hospital in Boston for psychotherapy every Wednesday afternoon during winter semester. The masters had a theory that I suffered from test-taking anxiety, and they thought a shrink could cure it. Years later I would be diagnosed with dyslexia. At that time, everyone figured that the source of my struggles must be emotional.

Thus began a period of snowy drives from Concord to Boston. It was a five-hour round trip, and it always interfered with my hockey practice, one of the few outlets I enjoyed during the winter. There was no way to get out of it. Although the rector never spoke the threat out loud, it was clear to me that I had to either go to therapy or be expelled from school.

Such a perverse contract was made more exciting when my dear friend Graham Wisner was shipped off to therapy with me. Graham was the last of four children born to Frank Wisner and Mary Ellis "Polly" Knowles. Polly was one of Washington's best-known socialites, a very close friend of my parents and Kay Graham, owner and publisher of the *Washington Post*. Frank served as one of the CIA's top-secret political operatives in Europe during the 1950s and early '60s.

During our sophomore year at St. Paul's, Frank committed suicide on the Wisner family farm in Maryland. As Graham experienced the finality, trauma, and sadness of completely losing his dad, I was beginning to experience the slow, forever-burning grief that enshrouded Robert McNamara's ongoing life.

We were just boys, fifteen years old, and we didn't know how to talk to each other about this sort of thing. In general, such intimate struggles were not openly discussed at St. Paul's. The idea there was to turn yourself into an increasingly bright and shiny object. So we went to therapy together. Every Wednesday afternoon, a Ford station wagon drove up to the schoolhouse to take us to Boston, and Graham hung out of his third-story window and shouted to anyone within earshot, "Time to go see the shrink, Craigie."

Once in Boston, we would take turns meeting with the psychiatrist. Graham quickly deduced that the shrink's secretary was also his wife. In an effort to put an end to the whole humiliating experience, he started to tell her amazing tall tales and outright lies while I was taking my turn on the psychiatrist's couch. Graham and I suspected that once we left, the secretary shared everything with her husband. Since the doctor sent a regular report back to the school, which in turn shared it with our parents, it didn't take long for Graham's tales to make their way back to Polly. Evidently one of the stories questioned her parenting skills. She was one of Washington's great society hostesses, known for bringing power couples together for intimate salon dinners, and I'm sure she became concerned about her reputation. The school reconsidered our weekly Boston appointments and eventually ended them.

"Bingo," Graham told me when we got the news. "No more therapy. A life lesson. After all, I was a spy's son."

Years later, as I was researching this episode of my St. Paul's experience, I discovered a confidential letter addressed to my parents from Dr. Leon Rosenberg, a Johns Hopkins child psychologist. He met with me on December 12, 1966, during Christmas vacation in my second year. His assessment was as follows:

> I would conclude from my examination that the youngster's test-taking anxiety and difficulty in mathematics do not constitute problems requiring psychotherapeutic intervention. I am certain that his high test anxiety is related to the demands of his school.... Therefore, if school authorities continue to stress the need for psychotherapy, I would recommend that the boy's parents remove him from the school.

I wonder if my father knew the depths of my academic failure, and I wonder what he thought about it. Maybe it embarrassed him. Then again, in 1966 he was probably thinking about managing the escalating war. If we had communicated openly back then, we might have shared our mutual feeling of being under enormous pressure. But we didn't talk about it, and no one in my life at that time seemed to give much thought to the possibility that the environment—the system—was the real problem.

Dr. Rosenberg's wish almost came true. I got close to being kicked out of St. Paul's several times. The administrators tried very hard to keep me on the right track. I was often summoned to Rector Warren's office. I remember trudging

11

through snow to the schoolhouse and climbing the steps to the second floor, slipping in my wet boots on the way up. His secretary greeted me outside the office. She always said something like "One minute, dear, while I get him." The tenderness of her voice put me at ease. She was one of the few women we schoolboys got to interact with, along with the masters' wives.

The rector's office was a peaceful study, not unlike the one adjacent to my parents' bedroom, where my mother used to help me with my homework and where my father did his taxes. The windows of that office faced out onto the snowy courtyard below, and Rector Warren kept a comfortable and warm space. Sitting in the chair across from him, I felt at rest. It was a pause from the competitions.

"Craig, I just had a phone call with your mother."

The calls to my parents were frequent. The letters the rector sent—some of which I have today—were often tender. I felt that the rector was a loving presence, and I could go to him for counsel. But that was his outer persona. The expectations he passed on were as clear as the edge of broken glass. Later, sometime after one of these meetings, the message came down from his office that I needed to repeat the tenth grade or leave.

It seems odd to me now that I chose to remain at the school. The place felt so repressive, so lonely, and so difficult. A few things helped. I managed to minimize the pain of my academic failings through camaraderie and friendships. The boys in the class I flunked out of didn't bully me; they remained my brothers. Academically, I learned how to cheat and take short cuts. I am certain that I plagiarized most of a paper on the topic "How Fidel Castro and Adolf Hitler

Compare as Instigators of Propaganda." As I recall, I lifted the content straight out of *Playboy*. I either didn't get caught, or they let me get away with it. This probably felt like a win at the time.

Other times, my mistakes caught up with me. One example was French class. All boys at the school had to take Latin in order to graduate. However, it soon became clear that I wasn't going to pass Latin. The rector allowed me to take French instead. I was happy about this, because French seemed romantic. The movie *A Man and a Woman* had just been released, and I was hopelessly in love with the actress Anouk Aimée. I even liked to listen to the movie's soundtrack on my record player. Certainly I was motivated. Unfortunately, French was not much easier than Latin. As the semester ground on and my grades tanked, I needed a short cut. Final exams were a week away. I could feel that tangy anxiety in my mouth, like when you touch the end of a double-A battery with your tongue. It was at that moment that the perfect solution occurred to me: just write the answers to the test questions on the cuff of my blue oxford.

I remember the schoolroom where we took the final exam. It had velvety forest-green curtains. I remember the windows, the bookshelves, and the hardness of the immovable seat on my backside. I can see myself there, wearing a long-sleeved shirt, tightly buttoned, perspiring heavily. Before long the ink began to run onto my hand. There went the test answers, down the river. I slowly unbuttoned my cuff to relieve the sweat.

I can't exactly recall what happened next. Did I answer the questions incorrectly? Did Monsieur Jacques notice the smudges of ink on my cuff? Whatever it was, I received an

F on the exam and spent the following June and July taking French in summer school.

Why did the school allow me so many chances? I really don't know. It could have been that the rector was patient. Certainly there was an attraction for the school in having the son of a cabinet member in its ranks. I credit my mother and father for not seeing themselves as celebrities and for keeping from my sisters and me any messages of entitlement. That doesn't mean we didn't get certain advantages.

Rock Gillespie and Bud Blake were my football and lacrosse coaches. They both came from working-class families, but sports had propelled them into the world of elite prep schools. With their crew cuts and no-bullshit attitudes, they were ideal mentors. I took their orders. I polished my football cleats just like Coach Rock instructed. I battled the black gnats that swarmed our late-summer practices. I cheered our team in victory and agonized with them in defeat.

Once, Mom and Dad came up to New Hampshire to watch a football game. They stood behind Coach Rock on our side of the field—the grown-ups as one entity, overseeing our pursuits. I remember Dad leaving the sideline several times to take phone calls. If this bothered me, I dealt with it by crushing a receiver from the other team. We managed to win the game, and afterward a few of my teammates came to dinner with us in town. I remember sitting next to Dad at the restaurant.

In his memoir, writing about this visit, Dad recalls a phone conversation with LBJ the night before the football game, in his hotel room. The conversation, he writes, concerned aluminum prices. In my memory, I feel certain that I saw Dad leave during the game to make a phone call. Whatever the case may be, he was clearly torn between his responsibilities as secretary of defense and his desire to be my father and watch me play. Maybe he was getting updates on Operation Rolling Thunder. Maybe the aluminum trade was important because we needed to manufacture more bomb casings. Who knows what orders my father approved while I was out on the field, tackling someone? I was just happy that my parents got to see us win. It was a disciplined afternoon on the gridiron, and we were rewarded with steaks and Cokes.

After a championship and an undefeated season, I was caught walking ten miles to a townie dance and spending an illegal night in town. I don't recall much about how I got there, where I spent the night, or whom I was with. Probably I was still chasing the promise I'd first heard back at Sidwell Friends—the beautiful girls, the sense of independence. It got me kicked off the football team, erasing the honor I'd won, which had done so much to make up for my other failures. Yet that recklessness ended up saving me from something worse, something I would have really regretted: a night with Cal Chapin.

Cal was one of the most unusual members of the St. Paul's community. Known by the boys as "Toad" for his lecherous laugh and round, toadlike face, Cal was the school's sex man. He graduated in 1935, and to the best of my knowledge, the school kept him on to entertain the jocks. In the parlance of the school, the student body consisted of the jocks, the flits, and the zeros. There was also a club on campus known as the "Porkers," and Cal was its faculty adviser. He recruited students who were good athletes and invited them to his apartment, where there was always plenty of "tea and toast," something that was coveted after a long football practice. I should know, because I was a Porker.

We all knew that Cal's real interest was taking boys to New York City over Thanksgiving or Christmas to go whoring. I don't think I realized at the time that Cal was the grand voyeur, taking pleasure from watching teenage boys have sex. We accepted this as another aspect of school, not considering what it meant for one of the school's adults to put us in this situation. In the fall of 1967, when I was seventeen, Toad asked me and another student to join him on a trip to New York at the beginning of Thanksgiving vacation. And then it happened: I was kicked off the football team for attending the townie dance. My punishment was to remain on campus for the first two days of Thanksgiving vacation, scraping gum off the bottom of school chairs. It was the luckiest punishment of my life. It saved me from a humiliating, degrading event.

How did I choose to go to this all-male school, where the term *Porker* was accepted? Looking back, I think single-sex education is incredibly unnatural, preventing young boys from seeing women as equals. *Porker* just seemed like a gross and funny word at the time. Now I feel ashamed at having ever uttered that word, knowing the way it was directed at women and sex workers. I feel anger on my own behalf too, at how the school allowed such abuse against its own students.

I feel that my life has been a journey outward. Maybe up, toward light. As a young teenager, I lived in the center of these dark institutions. It was so difficult not to see it all as normal. You tell yourself that it's not darkness; it's just the way things are. The known abyss.

Football was my way to escape the academic rigors of St. Paul's School.

In the late spring of 1968, when the campus air was sweet with lilacs, we saw the dream of Bobby Kennedy perish on TV. Just two months after the loss of Martin Luther King Jr., Bobby's death crushed me.

I had known him since the early 1960s. His son Joe, a few years younger than me, sometimes came over to our house. Joe and I often sat in my upstairs bedroom while Bobby and my father talked downstairs in the study. Joe and I played touch football at Hickory Hill, the Kennedy compound in McLean, Virginia. Bobby was competitive in family games, even to the point of being domineering. I couldn't have foreseen in those days that he would become a symbol and a spokesperson for peace, compassion, and the hope of progress.

Dad was chosen to be a pallbearer at Bobby's funeral, the same as he'd done when Jack Kennedy was killed. I felt I had to be there during this solemn occasion. But the school year had not yet ended. When I put in a request to attend the funeral, Rector Warren turned me down. To this day, the rigidity of his decision shocks me. For God's sake, this was not a political thing. This was about family and friends, a personal tragedy. And the school wasn't going to let me attend the funeral because I had used up all my free weekends? It seems so strange that the rector wouldn't budge on this issue. Maybe he thought the emotions of the funeral would impede my studies.

In the end, I just left. I hitchhiked sixty-eight miles to Boston, bought a plane ticket to Washington, and made it to the gravesite in time to see my father put Bobby to rest. I remember a cab ride somewhere along this journey. The cabbie asked me if I wanted to climb over the seat to sit next to him. After a few probing questions, I realized he wanted to have sex. At the next stoplight, I hopped out of the cab and walked the rest of the way to Arlington National Cemetery.

I think I recall catching my father's eye at the burial. I hadn't bothered to tell him I was coming, and he had no idea that I'd been able to leave school—much less that I had hitchhiked part of the way. As a pallbearer and participant in the ceremony, he couldn't reach out to me or acknowledge me. There were hundreds of people around us, but I feel strongly that we made each other out in the crowd, and I certainly remember his face. I saw deep sadness, loss beyond my comprehension. It was Bobby who a year earlier had said, "Bob, this war is unwinnable," encouraging Dad to end it. And now, a few months after he was released from his duties as secretary of defense, Dad was burying his friend—a man whose campaign for the presidency was based on ending the war in Vietnam—in the nation's cemetery for the war dead.

I wish there had been an invisible wire connecting Dad and me in our thoughts that night, some way we could have communicated our emotions without opening our mouths. Maybe an acknowledgment from me would have allowed him to be happier in his later years, to find fulfillment in his friends and family, to embrace his grandchildren.

It has been more than fifty years since Bobby's death. The pain is still with me. I came so close to my father that night. In a time and place of national mourning, as the late 1960s chipped further away at whatever innocence had survived boarding school, I almost reached him.

My tears won't stop.

2.

Our Sons Are Dying

The year I started boarding school, Norman Morrison stood beneath Dad's office window at the Pentagon, doused himself in kerosene, and self-immolated. His infant daughter, Emily, by his side.

Paul Hendrickson, who would go on to write meticulously and gracefully about my father's psyche, described Norman's death in an article in the *Washington Post:*

> He did it one rush-hour evening, in gathering dark, 40 feet below the window of the secretary of defense. The flame shot 12 feet in the air, making an envelope of color around his incinerating body. The sound of it, they said, was like the whoosh of small rocket fire....
>
> The public burning of Norman Morrison occurred in the gathering dark of a mistaken Asian war that Lyndon Johnson and all his steadfast men had lately, and mostly by stealth, made incendiary and even more mistaken. That summer, Vietnam had suddenly become a huge conflict, no longer the nice little one-column firefight

everybody thought it was going to be a few years earlier. There seemed to be no exit from the chosen path; 175,000 men were going in. American bombers had been raining destruction on the North since the previous February....

In the South, Buddhist monks had been immolating themselves for two years, but this burning seemed vastly different. It had occurred in our own civilization, right "at the cruel edge of your five-faced cathedral of violence." Those were a poet's words a few days afterward, and the poet must have had more in mind than the Pentagon itself. (Seven days later, a 22-year-old Catholic named Roger LaPorte would set himself afire at sunrise in front of the United Nations.) In the weeks and months following, there would be hundreds of poems pouring forth. It was as if only the poets could understand this thing Norman Morrison had made with his life. One poem was titled "Emily, My Child" and was written by a man named To Huu, one of the most famous poets in Vietnam. Another, addressing Defense head Robert S. McNamara, who was inside the five-faced cathedral that afternoon, began: "Mr. Secretary, you were looking another way / When grief stalked to your window to forgive you."

My office is a simple shed on my farm in Winters, California. When I sit at my desk, I look out my window at acres of walnut orchards. A few feet away from me, mostly unused, is Dad's rolling chair from the Pentagon. I can imagine Dad sitting in this chair when Norman burned himself alive. I picture Dad viewing that unfolding tragedy from his office, the most quotidian of settings, a place that in seven years I visited fewer than a handful of times. I can imagine his horror at witnessing a human life extinguished before his eyes. But the truth is that I don't even know if he looked. I have heard that he did; I'm not quite sure from whom, probably Paul Hendrickson. I didn't hear it from my father. He never said the name Norman Morrison to me, ever.

I was fifteen on November 2, 1965. I had arrived at St. Paul's School two months before Norman's death. At that time, I was attempting to adjust to the rigors and demands of my new environment. On that Tuesday evening, I suppose I was walking in the autumn twilight from my dorm to the dining hall. It would have been getting cold. I would have seen my breath in the light of the lamps around the grounds, the chapel, and the schoolhouse. I was passing through a dream of America's making, while a nightmare of my father's making unfolded many miles down the Eastern Seaboard.

Like so much about my father's life, I've had to understand this tragedy by reading other people's words—the words of journalists, historians, and essayists. It's very possible that the first time I ever heard about Norman Morrison was in 1985, when I read Paul Hendrickson's article in the *Post*.

I cried after reading about Norman—cried for the loss of that life, and for the loss of others represented by the act. For months afterward, the very breaths I took felt selfish. I felt ashamed to be alive. Today, having had many decades to process the emotions, I cry knowing that my shame and grief must have affected my family. Norman's daughter, Emily, was an infant at the time of his death. Many years later, my wife and I named our daughter Emily. Did I ever think about this connection?

Dad never talked to me about the time when a disgruntled protester tried to throw him off a Martha's Vineyard ferry. I found out about that on my own, again through reading. The absence of my real dad, and the overwhelming presence of so much historical material about him, make me imagine certain scenes from his life like moments from a play or movie. I am the director of my own fictional scenes, projecting a world. Had I been home in Washington after Norman's death, I imagine I would have witnessed a ghostlike version of Dad, with hunched shoulders and a pale face, bringing darkness with him through the heavy hickory doors of our home. Maybe his voice would have wavered while his left hand rubbed the tears from his eyes, dramatically, so that we, his audience, would know what he was feeling. Would I have hugged him, gently saying, *It's not your fault?*

What if Norman and Bob McNamara had actually met that day? Could Norman have persuaded my father to make different choices? Could the secretary of defense have dissuaded Norman from self-immolating? Would Dad have called me at boarding school, to tell me what happened?

All speculation.

One way or another, things pass through generations. Yet I can't remember one time when Dad spoke to me about his father, who died when Dad was in his late teens or early twenties. I didn't have a grandpa growing up, and I don't have many memories of my grandma either. I faintly remember her staying with us in Ann Arbor when I was six or seven years old. I recall an incident when I said something inappropriate in front of her, and she hauled me up to the tiled bathroom of our two-story Tudor home to wash my mouth out with soap. I often wonder if she treated my father this harshly. I don't think that Dad even attended her funeral. What kind of childhood brutalities did she inflict on him?

Books about my father fill in my family history, which should have been the task of the family itself. I should have heard from Dad about his upbringing during the Depression; I shouldn't have had to learn about it through second- and third-hand sources. At times, when I try to read books that go into our family history, I feel an emptiness spreading from my center. Parts of my body feel as though they're shutting down.

In certain writings and interviews, especially later in his life, my father stated that it was his intent to keep his family life separate from his career. He always tried to shield us. To an extent he succeeded in keeping his work as a statesman hidden. Even as a teenager, I never felt that I understood his daily routine or what his work consisted of. In fact, I didn't know the simplest things about his job—what motivated him to do it, and what aspects of his daily duties he enjoyed.

But try as he might, he couldn't always prevent the intrusion of reality. Etched in my memory is a series of eerie moments when the Bob McNamara shield cracked. I remember a ski trip to Aspen when I was in my early teens. It was Christmas vacation. After a day on the slopes, my parents' friends gathered in the ski lodge. They sipped cups of spiced tea and hot chocolate. A fire was blazing in the corner, drying our wet gloves and caps. One couple in the group were Quakers. They had assembled a seminar on the Vietnam War. They were dead set against the war, and they stood before the group, my parents included, and spoke with compassion about the need to end this violence. I don't remember my father's response.

However, I do have a memory of the expression on his face. He looked like a condemned man.

After the conversation, we all made our separate ways back to cabins and lodges, built little fires and turned the lights out before bed. I wanted Dad to acknowledge what happened. I wanted him to say to me, "Craigie, it will be all right." But he acted as if nothing had happened. Our lives resumed, and he continued to bury himself in the morning *New York Times* and *Washington Post*.

In those days, I didn't feel blame and resentment yet. Only grief. The controversy and tragedy in America during the mid-1960s suffocated us with grief just as much as they did the rest of the country. In my father's face and walk, even in his silence, I began to see flitting shadows of sadness. I didn't know it as a boy, but these were signs of depression, for which he would seek treatment later in life. It was during this time that my mother and I began to develop ulcers.

For most of my life I have attributed my ulcers to extreme stress. As a kid, school was my greatest source of stress. I remember crying uncontrollably over my homework, going back to at least the fifth grade. By the time I entered ninth grade, I had started to notice a biting, acidic feeling in my gut whenever I tried to struggle through any assignment based on reading or memorization. At boarding school, playing so many sports, I came to see my stomach pains as a point of honor, something to be endured in a manly way. I would grimace through them on the practice field. Riding in the front of the team bus, hyperfocused and competitive, I nearly forgot that I was hurting. Invariably, I would be clutching my stomach after the game was over, feeling that burn during the ride home.

In the mid-'60s, my mother and I went to see a Dr. Tumulty at Johns Hopkins. She and I had the same symptoms, and we were both diagnosed with ulcers. I assume we shared a genetic predisposition. More, I think that we both felt the weight of my father's decisions throughout our bodies and in every part of our minds. With a penchant for optimism, we never expressed our anguish in harsh words or self-abuse. Nor did we direct it at Dad. It all expressed itself in a more internal way. Dr. Tumulty advised us to drink more milk, and he prescribed a few drugs that didn't have much effect. I continued to feel pain from my ulcers well into college, where they sometimes had me doubled over as I walked from my dorm room to a class.

Dad must have known that we were suffering—especially Mom—throughout his time as secretary of defense. It must have worsened the pressures of his office. I imagine that every long working day and every difficult decision about Vietnam felt like an act combining courage, drudgery, and treason. The mere fact that he kept himself going during this time, that he didn't collapse in a hallway or pass out at his desk, is remarkable and disturbing. It takes a person with a certain misplaced strength to continue along a path that causes suffering and destroys lives—to know the costs and to continue all the same.

Dad left Defense in February of 1968. Depending on your interpretation of history, he either resigned or was fired, or a combination of both. I was approaching the end of boarding school, in a transition away from that repressive environment. It seemed that our family was coming to a new beginning.

On February 28, Dad was set to receive the Medal of Freedom from President Johnson in the East Room of the White House. I remember the whole ceremony as an almost religious experience; the light was coming in through the windows, pushing the dark out. At last we would be free from the war. Or so it seemed.

In a picture from that day, Dad holds the presentation box containing the medal. Over his left shoulder, my mother peers into the box, my oldest sister, Margy, at her side, my other sister, Kathleen, next to her. I am half out of the frame, the youngest kid by nine years and last in line, clapping my hands after the President concluded his remarks.

It was emotional for me to hear the President honor my father, and it must have been equally emotional for my sisters. LBJ and Lady Bird had attended Margy's wedding in 1965. I remembered the President's calm demeanor in the foyer of our home, socializing with wedding guests. Dad himself had given the commencement address at Kathleen's graduation from Chatham University, a then-all-women's college in Pennsylvania, as antiwar protesters demonstrated in front of the hall with signs that said "Bring our boys home so we can marry them."

Throughout our lives, my sisters and I have never talked about the ceremony in the East Room. In the picture, we look a bit like startled deer, unable to find our way back to some familiar pasture. If we could have gone there, to a quiet place of peace, we might have asked each other, *How are we going to live, knowing what our dad has done?* No such conversation ever took place, and that absence is a residual example of the pattern Dad had established with me: to go forth in life with a singular purpose, work hard, and shield family members from your innermost feelings.

However we all felt, the ceremony was certainly the most emotional for him. As Dad rose to receive the medal and make his speech, he broke down, unable to control his emotions. He coughed so that he wouldn't cry. In the shortest of moments, he stepped off the podium and into a new phase of his life.

In my family archives, I discovered a copy of a letter from Dad to President Johnson, dated just a few days before the ceremony. I believe that in this letter, Dad expresses some version of what he intended to say upon receiving the Medal of Freedom. The letter begins in true Bob McNamara style: "Fifty-one months ago you asked me to serve in your cabinet." Not "fifty months ago." Not "four years ago." Fifty-one.

The letter then takes a deep dive:

> *No other period in my life has brought so much struggle — or so much satisfaction. The struggle would have been infinitely greater and the satisfaction immeasurably less if I had not received your full support every step of the way.*
>
> *No man could fail to be proud of service in an administration which has recorded the progress yours has in the fields of civil rights, health, and education. One hundred years of neglect cannot be overcome overnight. You have pushed, dragged, and cajoled the nation into basic reforms from which my children and my children's children will benefit for decades to come. I know the price you have paid, both personally and politically. Every citizen of our land is in your debt.*

> *I will not say goodbye—you know you have but to call and
> I will respond.*

I'm amazed by the humility in these lines, which is to
a fault. Dad's attempts at sincerity pushed him far from his
own voice. When he uses words like *pushed*, *dragged*, and
cajoled, I feel as if I'm reading someone else's prose. These
sorts of words were unusual for my father. To me, they're
earthy words. I find them closer to references I would use on
my farm.

My father writes of how President Johnson's accomplish-
ments will matter for his "children's children." It's the sort of
stock phrase that politicians and public figures use. I'm sure
that these words don't stand out to many people who read
In Retrospect, the memoir in which Dad quotes this letter in
its entirety. But they stand out to me. Because his children's
children are my children.

My wife, Julie, and I purchased our farm in 1980. Dad
died in 2009, and I can count on one hand the number of
times he came and stayed with us on the farm. As a result, he
barely got to know my kids. He held them in his arms only
a few times. They're not just his children's children. They're
Graham, Sean, and Emily.

When my dad writes that he was not duplicitous to the
American people, I think he's ignoring a different truth. He
was duplicitous to himself. Maybe the pressures of his office
had required him to be absent from our lives, and to be
dishonest about what was really happening in Vietnam. But
why couldn't he make himself more present and honest once
he left office?

The journey we began as a family that February, which

could have been a journey to understanding one another in a life of peace, was never properly begun.

President Johnson presenting the Medal of Freedom to my father at the White House in 1968. As the youngest child, I'm standing the farthest away. (Yoichi R. Okamoto)

There were many conversations I didn't have with my father about Vietnam. There is one that I did have. After he published *In Retrospect* in 1995, I went to visit him in Washington. Dad was still living in the house where I grew up: 2412 Tracy Place NW.

After dinner we began chatting over drinks in what he called the "Green Room," which was his study. We talked about the enormous blowback caused by his memoir. I hadn't read it—at that time, I hadn't read the vast majority of my father's writings—but I understood from media coverage that his latest book, the first in which he truly addressed his controversial role in Vietnam, had not garnered the reception he had hoped for. Although Dad felt that he had admitted his mistakes, veterans who reviewed the book thought he stopped short of apologizing. In the pages of the *Washington Post*, Ron Kovic (author of *Born on the Fourth of July*) had written passionately about wanting Robert McNamara to understand the true cost of the war, which could not be calculated in lessons learned but in lost limbs and lives.

Ron lived in California. After his review was published, I called him and spoke with him. I wanted to feel fully his justified anger. I wanted to know the pain that veterans were feeling. Speaking with Ron, I understood that he wanted to welcome my father into the community of people who could understand, acknowledge, and feel the irreparable harm of the war—people who were wounded. So why wouldn't Dad have that conversation? Why wouldn't he meet with someone like Ron? This was a duty he owed veterans.

Dad and I went on a walk around the neighborhood. The conversation changed. It had been about the book; now it was becoming about us. I had an aggressive posture that evening, and I was more demanding than I'd ever been. We kept our voices down—this was an elite DC neighborhood, after all—but I was still brutally honest with him.

"I guess they're mad because it took you thirty years, Dad."

His views on this never changed. "You have to remember, I was acting from my experience in history."

"And you still acted wrong."

These were the most probing things I ever said to him. My words were heartfelt, not strategic. Later in life, when I desperately wanted to have a more complete conversation about Vietnam, I think Dad could sense this in me, and he was better able to deflect the subject.

At one point I asked him, "Dad, why did it take you so long?"

What he said still causes me to pause.

"Loyalty."

I might have said to him, *Why can't you be loyal to me, Dad? Or to yourself? What about the people who died? What about that loyalty?*

I never asked him that first question, about loyalty to me, but I wish I had. That night I was trying to get him to say *I'm sorry* for Vietnam. I believed he should have apologized more fully. But Dad couldn't do it. He ended the conversation by talking about himself in a vaguely repentant but unapologetic way.

"I made mistakes, Craigie."

Loyalty, for him, surpassed good judgment. It might have surpassed any other moral principle. Dad was loyal to John F. Kennedy and Lyndon Johnson, and that loyalty had many consequences. He came to be personally identified with the Vietnam War. At times I thought this was unfair. Out of a desire to defend him, I sometimes made excuses. He was just one of many people responsible; he was underqualified for the job; his business background and statistical fluency made him a perfect symbol for the hated military-industrial complex, the great machine. It wasn't all his fault.

But he didn't speak up enough when he knew the war couldn't be won. While in office, he repeatedly told the public that we were making progress in Vietnam—that victory was just around the corner. For years afterward, he deflected questions about his Vietnam leadership, undermining the truth by refusing to take responsibility for policies that had horrific consequences. Whether it was the use of

Agent Orange, the bombing campaigns that killed millions of civilians, or the faulty statistics he relied on, Dad didn't admit to his mistakes when doing so could have changed history. He always hid behind simplistic words like those from his memoir—*we were wrong, we made mistakes.*

His loyalty was a kind of corporate loyalty. Regardless of the consequences for ordinary people, Dad stayed loyal to the system. He may have believed that he was only part of the system that caused the war, but he was still one of the nation's most prominent leaders, one of the few with the capacity to reshape policy with his leadership and intellect. If he thought the war was wrong but couldn't buck the system, then he should have left that system. He did not. Instead, he waged war. Afterward, he didn't say he was sorry. To me, this is the truth about his loyalty.

Meanwhile, Dad's loyalty provided him with many personal advantages. After his departure from Defense, he stepped into a career as head of the World Bank. He spent the next twelve years visiting practically every country and prime minister in the world. A global dignitary, he never had to suffer the consequences of losing a war. In other countries, countries that aren't the American Empire, the losers of wars are executed or exiled or imprisoned. Not so for Robert McNamara.

After my mom died in 1981, the boards of Dutch Shell Oil, Bank of America, the *Washington Post*, and the Rockefeller Foundation wined and dined Dad, flying him all over the world to consult on the cutting issues of the time. His confidants were Jackie Kennedy, Kay Graham, Ted Kennedy, and President Bill Clinton. The firm Corning Glass gave him a handsome corner office in Washington, where he had a magnificent glass globe. Each and every one of his friends, in and out of government, appreciated his loyalty to them. Though he never bragged about his captainship of global intelligentsia and trade, I know that he liked it. He often told me how much he enjoyed flying from Boston to London to attend meetings, because he could see Martha's Vineyard out the window of the plane.

Did I benefit from Dad's loyalty? In many ways I did. On climbing trips, we were literally tethered to the same rope as we ascended Mt. Rainier or rappelled down the face of Grand Teton. Yes, he was loyal.

And I have been loyal to him. In his final months and days, I bathed him and dressed him. I have sometimes worried that I treated him too generously, especially in interviews and in writing, handling him with kid gloves. It's hard to be objective. Goddammit, this is my father we're talking about: caretaker, loving dad, hiking buddy—obfuscator, neglectful parent, warmonger.

In February of 1968, the month of Dad's retirement from Defense, my St. Paul's classmate Cam Kerry wrote an op-ed in our school newspaper, *The Pelican*.

> We are trying to win the unwinnable war, like Don Quixote, "to dream the impossible dream," and like Don Quixote, we are doomed to tilt at windmills.

At the time he penned this op-ed, Cam was only seventeen years old. His brother John Kerry was commanding a Swift Boat in Vietnam.

The clarity of Cam's conviction amazes me today. When I was at boarding school, I didn't realize how politicized and informed many of my peers were about the war. Cam managed to express himself in such certain and powerful terms in a public forum. At around this same time, I stood in the East Room of the White House meekly, watching my dad receive the Medal of Freedom, feeling a mixture of pride, embarrassment, amazement, and discomfort, with uncertainty as to the proportion of each emotion.

Where was the op-ed that I might have written? At that point I still couldn't string sentences together for a term paper. Instead, I was on page seven of the March 12, 1968, edition of *The Pelican* in a story about sports. "McNamara Wins in School Wrestling Tourney." I wasn't even on the wrestling team. There had been an open tournament, and I gave it a go, channeling my energies toward these light competitions while some of my peers were trying to make themselves heard.

I didn't express myself at boarding school, but in my bedroom at home during the summers, where my father might see them, I began my earliest protests. On the third floor of our home on Tracy Place, I hung the American flag upside down on the wall above my bed. After that, I stamped my letters with the upside-down American flag. I imagined the mail carrier looking at the outside of my letters and knowing that someone in the McNamara house wasn't for the war.

These were vulnerable years for me as the youngest child in the family. I experienced that unique window of time, uncomfortable and powerful in its intimacy, reserved for the last child remaining in the house. Even without the Vietnam War, this would have been a period of reshaping my relationship with my parents. It coincided with the beginnings of a national (and international) nightmare.

Returning from Vietnam, Dad would bring home certain artifacts. These included rifles, pistols, flags, and other objects from the field of battle. They were not souvenirs, nor trophies; I think that Dad was interested in them as historical and cultural keepsakes. Throughout his life he collected objects from overseas, including during his travel as president of the World Bank. I soon developed a complex relationship with these Vietnam artifacts. Without telling him, I pilfered them from wherever he had deposited them (probably his closet or study), put them up in my bedroom, and made them a part of my living space. Viet Cong flags hung on my walls. One flag was captured from the battle of Dai Do. It had been taken from a firefight in which US forces and the North Vietnamese army slaughtered each other in rice fields. I also had a collection of confiscated guns and bullets. Punji stakes adorned my shelves. These bamboo stakes were as sharp as razors and barbed in two places. They were used by the Viet Cong as traps—dipped in human feces, then placed in camouflaged pits. The idea was not necessarily to kill the soldier but rather to cause a wound that required medical evacuation by helicopter.

The decorations on a teenage boy's walls don't hold any great secrets. As a younger teenager, fourteen or fifteen years old, I probably felt a fascination with foreign guns. Eventually, I started to recognize the horror of those weapons, and it matched the discomfort I felt about the war. When I was sixteen and seventeen and growing in my understanding, the Viet Cong flags came to represent a protest against my father. My response to the war may not have been an intellectual or an editorial one, but my feelings about the war were becoming stronger every day.

My father never acknowledged what was going on in my bedroom. Certainly he never brought it up. My mother, on the other hand, tried to temper my protests, which must have been seen by Dad as painful insults. She often ascended the carpeted stairway to my room. In her gentle voice, Pacific-blue eyes shining, she'd ask me something about my life. Did I feel confident in my classes at school? How were my friends doing? Was the pain from my ulcers any less severe?

In response, I would try to deflect and comfort her. "How are you doing, Mom? I'm doing fine."

I remember Mom pleading with me, "Just give your father another chance. Keep trying."

She probably said something similar to Dad. "He's just expressing himself. He's saying how he feels."

How can you open the door to someone who won't walk through?

This story of absence is the same story told about many fathers and sons. With my father, there's also the question of evil.

There was an afternoon in 1979 when I went to the Tower Theatre in downtown Sacramento with Julie—my girlfriend and future wife—and my mother. At the time, we were renting a house in the countryside around Winters. Mom was staying with us. After some casual conversation, the three of us decided to have an evening at the movies. *Apocalypse Now* was playing.

It must have been late summer, shortly after the film premiered. I can't remember if I thought about the consequences of taking Mom to see a Vietnam War film. I do remember that the hype around *Apocalypse Now* was significant. Perhaps I was the driving force for this. Maybe I thought it was a way for us to close out that chapter of our lives—to view a tragedy in the theater, to experience a catharsis.

I distinctly remember where we sat: midsection, about fifteen rows back, just under the vintage chandeliers. Mom sat between Julie and me. I don't remember any tension in her posture. Then the room went dark. The soundtrack began, with Jim Morrison singing "The End." Immediately I went deep into my own thoughts and feelings. The end of my mother's life was not far away; she would die from cancer in 1981. The war had ended six years before, and my father's tenure in government had also ended. Thoughts of so many endings overwhelmed me when I heard that song, and I felt myself losing breath, my chest tightening, like the feeling just before a sob is released. Only there was no release. As the movie played, and the violence mounted, I realized that this wasn't an ending at all. The Vietnam War would continue to have profound implications for the country, my family, and me for years to come. We were just coming to the beginning—the beginning of the rest of our lives. There was a strongly felt, deeply personal sense of irony in hearing the words *This is the end* over the opening frames.

As we sat in the dark theater, I didn't touch Mom. I glanced at her a few times to see her expression, and it was stoic. Crying was rare for her. She wore a coping face. I wonder what she was thinking about. I imagine she was horrified as we watched American helicopters rain down death and destruction during the Ride of the Valkyries scene. She and I are so similar, and we certainly are in this respect: we don't like violence.

Taking my mother to the film was what Dad would have called "a god-awful mess." More than that, it was a living nightmare. Why did I think it was a good idea? What could my mom have possibly gained from this experience besides despair and remorse? If she felt any relief that her husband's active role in the war was over, perhaps that experience reopened an old wound for her. Maybe the ulcer in her gut writhed as the onscreen gunships spewed their bullets at innocent children. Did she mourn for the American dead, wondering if her own son should have served?

I honestly don't remember what we did after the movie. I suppose we went out to eat, although it's hard to imagine being hungry after watching *Apocalypse Now*. I'm sure that at some point, probably over dinner, I said, "Mom, I'm sorry."

It would have been nice if my father had said these words. Again, that duty fell to me. And it was about a movie—an interpretation of his actions, far removed from him and from the victims of the actual war—not the real thing. I wonder if she told him about that night. I wonder if he was angry at me for taking her to the movie. I wonder if they even talked about it.

Recently I rewatched the trailer for the film. I immediately experienced the same dread I felt in 1979 when I sat next to my mom in the dark theater. At first I thought that I should watch the whole movie again, but after viewing several more trailers, I said to myself, *Fuck, no*. I don't need to see any more representations of Vietnam War massacres. These fictional responses to my father's war are inadequate to describe the magnitude of what he delivered to the world.

But what would be adequate? I think of all the unexploded ordnance in Vietnam, the lingering effects of chemical warfare, and I realize that the aftereffects will outlive not only my father but also me.

It's not that I think he could have made up for his mistakes. What bothers me is that he didn't make a sufficient effort. It took him decades just to admit that he made mistakes. Because of that fact, movies became one of the only ways for me to understand Vietnam with a degree of objectivity. As a noncombatant, I am limited in my understanding, informed by receiving literary and narrative interpretations. In that respect I am not unique; I share that experience with millions of other people. Yet I am unique in being the son of the war's architect.

3.

The Angel of the House

How can a family never speak the truth, despite having good and comfortable lives?

My memories of our home are pleasant, with only occasional smudges of darkness, like spots and scratches on a film reel. As a child I was allowed to go into my parents' bedroom and bathroom. They always had twin beds, with a shared headboard. I liked to raid their drawers and dressers for coins. I'm not sure what I wanted to buy with the loot. They never noticed it was missing. In their bathroom I sometimes found the case for a rubber mouth guard, my father's. He ground his teeth at night. Their medicine cabinet was filled with drugs to treat my mother's ailments.

She had night terrors. These started when we moved from Ann Arbor to Washington. She never told me about them directly, other than to say, "I had a bad dream, Craigie." She didn't confide in me what her bad dreams were about. I have a few guesses.

When she was young, after my sisters were born but before I was born, Mom spent a year in an iron lung. She'd

41

contracted polio. Dad got it too. During that time, he was stationed in Salina, Kansas, where he was serving in the Air Force's strategic bomber unit. My parents were quarantined. They had no support system in place in Salina, so my older sisters (ages five and two) were sent to live with relatives in Toronto and San Francisco. I have to believe that this experience affected the whole family. Although Dad himself had only a mild case of polio, he later said that concerns about my mother's medical expenses influenced his decision to work at the Ford Motor Company (as opposed to pursuing an academic career). Mom, meanwhile, never talked about her horrific confinement. I wish I had asked her about it. I always knew that she loved wide-open spaces, hiking, and swimming. Probably she appreciated her body enormously after nearly losing her mobility.

For Mom, the 1950s were a reprieve from sickness and from the convulsions of World War II. In those years, when we lived in Ann Arbor, my parents' friends included Ford executives, university professors, artists, and doctors. The McNamaras were a cool, intellectual couple who loved hosting book club. She was a great hostess, and I remember her many elaborate Halloween parties. Mom would dress up as Morticia and Dad as Lurch from the 1950s Charles Addams cartoons. The black-and-white photos of these couple costumes are striking to look at today; my parents both look more unguarded and natural than during the Washington days, when Mom went through a frumpy phase and Dad aged a hundred years. I have other photos in which they reenacted a radio studio together, complete with microphone sets, wigs, and makeup. These are some of the only pictures I have where my father isn't sporting his signature, severe hairdo.

I remember saying goodbye at the door as my parents went out to a Halloween cocktail party. Mom was carrying a clear vinyl purse with a live rat in it. I remember her doing the same thing with a baby alligator. Where did she get these live props? They showed her fascination with biology and nature. During the week, while Dad was commuting to Ford corporate headquarters in the posh community of Dearborn, Mom and I would head down to the local slaughterhouse on the other side of the train tracks dividing Ann Arbor. There, she would pick up cow lungs, brains, and eyeballs to bring home for hands-on biology lessons. When she was an undergraduate at Cal Berkeley, where she had met my father, the bio lab had been her favorite class. She liked to instruct me in the science of dissection. Once home from the slaughterhouse, we'd sit at the kitchen counter, scalpels in hand, and begin the delicate process of removing layers of the cow's eyeball. She would neatly place the cornea, optic nerve, iris, and aqueous humor on a tray in front of us. Once we had filleted the eyeball, Mom pulled out her dissection microscope to give me a closer look at how the fragile parts of the eye worked together. The lungs were my favorite organ to dissect, because Mom would stick plastic straws into the airless trachea of the spongy pink sacs, and together we'd blow air into the tubular branches of the bronchi. Whenever we stopped blowing, the lungs made a hissing sound as the air rushed out.

Maybe she thought I'd become a doctor, surgeon, or some kind of scientist. There were many nights when she tried to help me with my homework. We would sit in the den just off their bedroom, and I would cry as I struggled.

To me she was the essence of Mother Nature, embodying life-giving and nurturing qualities. Her sense of comfort rubbed off on Dad too. He came to appreciate nature in part because of her. Well into my thirties and forties, he and I would skinny-dip together after his early-morning runs to the beach on Martha's Vineyard. He would run down the oak-lined path with only a T-shirt on, carrying his thermometer to take the ocean temperature so that he could announce it over breakfast. Once, long after Mom died, we were hiking up to Snowmass Lake in the Colorado Rockies. Just under Buckskin Pass, we came to the place where we had buried Mom's ashes, in a bronze tube that I had crafted on the farm. As we arrived at her resting place near a weathered, twisted old pine tree, Dad declared, "That's right where your mother and I camped…and made love together."

Oh boy. That was more than I bargained for. Yet I felt close to him. More power to the two of them, I thought, for loving each other in one of nature's most beautiful valleys.

It was so easy to be in Mom's space, less so in Dad's. Mom and I rarely fought. One time, when I knew she was listening in on a hot phone conversation I was having with a girlfriend, I felt angry at her. When she came upstairs and knocked on my door, I ignored her. She called out my name, "Craigie?," and I grumbled something about being tired. That may be the angriest I ever got at her. I probably apologized later. I don't think we agonized over it very much. I loved her, and I couldn't stay mad. Even when she was intrusive, nothing could be her fault. That's how it felt.

Her world shifted significantly after the 1960 election. I remember the day things changed. Dad arrived home from his commute and asked me, "What would you think about moving to Washington, Craigie?" I was loving life: running

44

away from school, catching frogs, making dams in the creek behind the house. I didn't know if Washington had these things. The prospect of moving must have been even more unsettling for my middle sister, Kathleen, who was in high school at the time.

I knew what to say to my parents. With my best ten-year-old reasoning, I told them, "No thanks, I've got my friends and my tree house right here. I'm not going!"

Surely it was Mom who broke the news to me. The news being that I had no choice in this matter. She probably added, "It will be an adventure."

From her perspective, the new position must have been an improvement. I remember Dad enjoying his work and his commute (which he made in a stylish aqua-blue Thunderbird), but I'm not sure how Mom felt about being married to a car executive. That industry, and all the Republicans in it, must have contrasted with her love of nature and her politics. The draw of the Kennedys and the excitement of Camelot must have seemed to present a dynamic and bright future. It was Sargent Shriver, JFK's brother-in-law, who called Dad on behalf of the President-elect. The story goes that he asked my father to choose between being secretary of the treasury and secretary of defense. As a child I didn't appreciate the gravity of the call; as an adult, I can imagine what it must have felt like. Over my career, I have fantasized about serving in government, maybe as secretary of agriculture. It would be intoxicating.

Part of me wishes that Dad had turned it down, or that Mom had made him refuse. I know what I would have done in his shoes. If some person had called me years ago with an opportunity that took me away from the life I've built, the one I'm still living, the part of me that comes from Mom would have supported the temptation.

Diagnosed with terminal mesothelioma, my mother continued her adventures in the outdoors during the last months of her life.

I was ten years old when we moved. I stood on the steps of the US Capitol on a cobalt-blue Friday morning in January of 1961, when JFK spoke his now famous words: "Ask not what your country can do for you, ask what you can do for your country." At home, we often quoted the verse from Luke: "To those to whom much has been given, much is required." For our family, service was an ideal to strive for.

Looking back, I think those years required the most service from Mom. Going from being the wife of the president of Ford Motor Company to the wife of the secretary of defense changed the trajectory of her life, and she had to adjust accordingly. Early on, President Kennedy arranged a meeting of the cabinet wives, where he encouraged them to dedicate themselves to something productive, since their husbands would be working long hours in government. Never mind that they were already being productive, keeping their families afloat.

I can't relate to the pain of her anonymity. Receiving none of the shiny public glory of those early Camelot days, she was the one who held us together. Upon arriving in Washington, she did everything she could to normalize our lives. She worked to make sure we weren't around "society" and that we didn't notice security people and fancy diplomatic proceedings, the trappings of power.

One of Mom's dearest friends was Lydia Katzenbach. Lydia's husband, Nick, served as the deputy attorney general. In June of 1963, he had confronted Alabama governor George Wallace on the steps of the University of Alabama. That was just six months after my father was facing the political fallout of the Cuban Missile Crisis. Dad and Nick were regularly criticized and even faced death threats. One day, my eighth-grade history and homeroom teacher, Harvey LeSure, told me that my father had narrowly escaped an assassination attempt while traveling to Vietnam.

When I got home that day, I hugged my mom and told her about what the history teacher had said. She wasn't angry, and she didn't show any fear. She reminded me that Dad was all right, that he was coming home. It didn't occur to me to ask anything else. It seemed natural that my parents would protect me.

There must have been a real sting to certain inequities of their marriage: having to cook his meals, arrange his evening wear; having to stay silent around the kids and not voice the fear that he would be shot or that we would all die in a nuclear attack. She supported him through his moral downfall in the 1970s, when there were still people who wanted him dead (some of his countrymen too), because her role was to give and to nurture—and because she really was a giving and nurturing person.

There were exciting things for Mom too, things that intoxicated her. She loved going out. When they weren't parenting, Mom and Lydia took DC by storm. I remember the many occasions when they met at our house before going to some official dinner or diplomatic cocktail party. Lydia wore her beautiful hair in a beehive tilted slightly backward. It resembled the nose of a B-52 bomber. My mom went everywhere with her Kodak automatic camera around her neck, shooting many photos of presidents and prime ministers. She also used that camera to document civil rights demonstrations at the Capitol.

Lydia and Mom were intrigued by the idea of conspiracy. They got to imagining that every phone conversation was bugged. On one of their many chats, they both heard shuffling noises, and then a band struck up "The Star-Spangled Banner" in the background as they talked. For years they were convinced that they had a "patriotic companion" listening in on their calls. One day Mom thought their eavesdropper friend must be very bored by their conversations, and she suggested to Lydia that they should liven up his dull days.

From then on, they brightened their talks with fanciful tales and tidbits—all totally fictitious—about Washington society and imaginary friends and neighbors. They were convinced that somewhere in the data collections these tall tales were buried and that they would be dug up in the future and mistaken for truth and history. Of course, it's possible that none of this was a joke. The FBI bugged hundreds of people in the early '60s. Why not us?

I remember a machine we had in the coatroom of our house, just off the entry hallway. The "scrambler" was a behemoth of a device, steel-gray, tucked away in a not-very-secure closet. I can't remember exactly when the scrambler was installed, but it must have been shortly after we moved into our home on Tracy Place. The purpose of the scrambler was to keep my father's communications secret during events like the Cuban Missile Crisis. It was wired to a gray plastic telephone on his bedside table, one floor above the coatroom closet. The phone resembled a typical rotary-style model of the times, but it didn't have a dial. Rather, there was a red plastic light on the receiver, the kind I had on my Lionel train transformer. I remember being tempted to pick up the phone to see who answered it, but I was afraid I would set off an alarm and start a nuclear attack. The scrambler, I assume, was a device designed to prevent spies from hacking the line and discovering in advance the position of the secretary of defense.

Mom slept a few feet away from the scrambler phone. Somewhere beneath her bed, beneath the floor, was a connection in which the balance of the world rested. At night, she was close to this physical symbol of global security—or insecurity. Meanwhile, my bedroom was probably thirty feet away from the scrambler phone. History intruded on our sleep. No wonder she had nightmares. No wonder I see her in myself.

Mom suffered from so many ailments. There was a duodenal ulcer, and several painful operations to repair it. Rheumatoid arthritis bent her fingers into a beggar's hands. I'm sure there were more wounds in her life than I know about.

Yet her career—the career she was able to have—was dedicated to improving the lives of others. With a Ford Foundation grant, she started a nonprofit called Reading Is Fundamental, which helped deliver books to children in the DC public schools. I have fond memories of her early bookmobiles, milk trucks converted into mobile libraries.

She pushed the boundaries of domestic life during our outdoor adventures. I remember a time when we were camping in Colorado. With the temperature below freezing, she wanted to bring the dog into the tent. Dad wasn't having anything to do with that. He tolerated dogs, but he didn't like them. Mom said, "Either the dog sleeps with us, or I sleep outside." Bingo. It was actually one of the few times I can remember her giving him what-for.

I remember fishing with her on our Sierra trips. She was the one who taught me to tie a fly on the end of a line and fish for golden trout. Dad stayed behind at the campsite as we bushwhacked to an alpine lake. He wasn't a fisherman. When just the two of us were fishing, she must have experienced a kind of freedom, brief but necessary, from him.

In March of 1981, a month after Mom's death, I returned to Washington to visit Dad. I can't say whether he had changed with her passing. I think what he felt then was a combination of grief and relief after her long illness.

One morning we headed off to play tennis in Bethesda. It was a typical DC winter day: slushy, dirty snow along the road, fog clinging to the trees, cold in the air—colder still in our somber spirits. We entered the bubble dome, walked onto the court, and quietly rallied to warm up.

Mom and Dad had played a lot of tennis together. Playing with him was a comforting act on my part. I thought it would ease the pain of losing her, at least for the morning. As we took a few soft serves, I bit my lip and thought about the game we were about to play.

Every marriage has its unique balancing acts, and in their marriage, one of these was my Mom's willingness to let Dad beat her in tennis. They were both good athletes, but she had superior hand-eye coordination. She could beat him most of the time, but she would invariably fake a serve into the net and let him win. As Dad and I started to play a set that day, I readied myself to perform the old ritual. I was Mom. I dinked a forehand out of bounds and let him beat me. Imagining myself in her role, I wondered why this was necessary. Was it to make Dad feel superior and in control? Did such fakery really keep their marriage together?

Losing on purpose is like not telling the truth. I'm competitive, and I consider myself honest, so our charade hurt me disproportionately. I did it out of love for my dad. I loved him so much. I let him get away with it.

Throwing a family game is not comparable to misleading Congress, the press, and the American people about the winnability of the Vietnam War. There's a difference in magnitude, obviously. But it shows that even my mother, who was such an amazing partner, couldn't always arrive at honesty with him. I've thought of her with some sadness as an enabler of his worst qualities. Maybe he was simply too egotistical and overpowering. He certainly was a dictator in the office, snapping at people and harshly criticizing their mistakes. Who knows if it has anything to do with tennis? Things get stuffy in marriages. Assumptions are made that ought to be thrown asunder.

After our game, Dad and I made our way back to the old house at 2412 Tracy Place. We had a halting conversation on the way home. Dad asked, "How are you and Julie?"

This was a bit out of the ordinary. He almost never asked me about my marriage. I responded that, all in all, Julie and I were well. I said, "We have a few problems, but everyone does."

There was a long pause, ended by my father's comment: "Your mother and I never had any problems."

Perhaps now that their time together was over, he had started to develop a selective memory. It might even have felt true, if she always let him win at things.

During many difficult years, Mom had served as a conduit for communication between Dad and me. When she was gone, there was an opportunity for us to grow closer. It didn't really happen. He guarded the lines closely, limiting the topics we could address out loud as much as he ever had. And now I felt that I had lost my translator. My first, last, and only way of seeking some insight into the depths of his heart.

4.

Absence, Defense

I remember, as early as age thirteen, having questions about my father's integrity. He had numerous conflicts with members of Congress, and the press gobbled it up. An article from *Newsweek* published in March of 1963 describes his reputation:

> With cold logic and a hot temper, Secretary McNamara took on congressmen last week in two fractious issues: the size and nature of the defense budget, and the huge (ultimately $6.5 billion) TFX aircraft contract. His opposition's allies, barely behind the scenes, were the enemies McNamara has liberally made as a tough, head-knocking executive.

The article goes on to discuss the various things about Dad that bothered the pols: his arrogance, his condescending tone, and (most of all) his willingness to circumvent bureaucratic processes in order to get his own way.

At one point, my mother addressed this with me. I can't

pinpoint the exact moment—which news story or national event prompted her to sit down and talk to me. I only remember that she came into my bedroom and explained that I might be hearing negative things about Dad. Later, during one of Dad's congressional dustups, I spoke with a reporter. Again, it must have been my mother who allowed me to talk to the press. I would have sat in the living room on the phone, with Mom nearby or in the next room, listening in. When I spoke to the reporter, I asked, "How long will it take my father to prove that he's honest?"

Soon after this quote appeared in print, I received a dozen letters from across the country. They vouched for my father's character. Among them was a letter from Vermont congressman Robert Stafford, a former governor and future senator. On his official stationery he wrote, "I have had the privilege of observing your father for the last three years as he appeared before the House Armed Services Committee. I have come to hold tremendous admiration for his ability, judgment, and integrity. I think he is one of the ablest public servants with which this country has been blessed."

Another letter, penned by a serviceman, read, "I wanted you to know that for me and for many thousands of other people, there is no question about your father's honesty, or anything else about him. He is a great man doing great work. He is serving his country with a courage and devotion just like that of George Washington, Thomas Jefferson and Abraham Lincoln."

Before I dug up that *Newsweek* article from March of 1963, I remembered having been quoted in it. This was not the case; my name didn't appear. I must have spoken to a different reporter for a different article. What I remember more clearly, and very painfully, is finding out for the first time that my father was fallible, that his shield could be broken, and that he might not be the titan of my childhood. How could anyone attack his integrity? It must be a mistake. But then, how could he make a mistake? I was distraught.

It comforted me to know that a congressman, a member of the military, and private citizens viewed my father as a man of integrity. Getting those letters allowed me to consciously return to a state of innocence, where I could trust him. He would do the right thing. In retrospect, maybe it would have been better if those letters hadn't come. Maybe it would have helped me to arrive earlier at the conclusion that my father's life was not lived wholly on the righteous path. Maybe it would have saved me from the mind-bending pain of those years when I discovered I had been living in the shadow of dishonesty.

Two decades later, in the spring of 1984, David Talbot wrote an article for *Mother Jones*, "And Now They Are Doves." The article covered my father's attempts to rehabilitate his image and step into the role of elder statesman. At that time, I was thirty-four years old, farming my heart out. I had a wife and child.

Over the years, I had thought about Dad every day with a mixture of love and rage. Whenever we spoke and I asked him about Vietnam, he deflected. There was never a big confrontation between us. I remember my life at that time as being defined by an absence of truth and honesty in our relationship, and I remember how I had defended Dad's integrity when I was a boy—and the letters from his supporters too.

David Talbot called and suggested an interview, and it felt like an opportunity I needed to take. I didn't want the media attention. I just wanted the chance to speak honestly, to be heard. David came to visit the farm in Winters, and we spoke for an afternoon. Earlier that day, I'd been on the phone with Dad, updating him on the progress of our orchards.

The published article in *Mother Jones* included a lengthy quote from me. I had never criticized my father so publicly.

There had to be a lot of guilt and depression inside my father about Vietnam. But he will not allow me into the personal side of his career. My father has a strong sense of what he will and won't talk about with me. I would ask him things, like why he left the Pentagon in '68. I felt I could learn a tremendous amount of history from him. And I felt I could teach him about the peace movement. But he just gives these quick 30-second responses, and then deflects the conversation by asking, "So how many tons did you produce on your farm last year?" Still seeking refuge in statistics.

I didn't know if Dad would read the article. One of the many mysteries that remained was the extent to which he followed his own publicity. If I had taken the time to think about it carefully, I probably would have concluded that he did. After all, I knew of his ego and his need to be right, to win.

He called me up almost immediately after the piece ran.

"Is that what you said?" he asked. "Was the quote correct?"

I was a little surprised by the quick timing, but I wasn't surprised by his response. If anything, it confirmed my disappointment in him. It showed that he cared about his own narrative, when he should have just driven himself hard to the unspun truth.

"Yeah, Dad," I said. "The quote was correct."

He was silent. This was always the way he reacted to being hurt. I knew I had hit him in a tender place. I felt sad, but I didn't feel sorry. It was the first time I had offered my version of the truth and the first time he had heard it.

After a little time had passed, my stance softened. I reread the *Mother Jones* article several times and convinced myself that it was full of errors and omissions, and I started to believe that David Talbot had neglected important truths about my relationship with Dad—especially the fact, unavoidable, that we loved each other deeply.

I wanted Dad to know how I was feeling. In a follow-up letter to him, I wrote, "They failed to say that we have a relationship based on understanding."

I really believed that, but it wasn't the truth. Our relationship was, in fact, based on joy and affection when it came to the things we shared, and deliberate silence and absence relating to the issues of war and peace that divided us. If we had really had a relationship based on understanding, there's no way I would have given that quote about his thirty-second responses.

As I reread the article today, I see that there were no errors. David Talbot didn't misquote me or misrepresent my views. I was serious when I told him that I believed the power brokers in Washington, including my father, had made decisions in Vietnam based solely on the military interests of America. So why did I reverse course in private? I think I was reenacting the pattern Dad had established, the one I had learned to follow. I thought I could hold two truths in my head at once, in separate cages, without working through the dialectic. I love you, Dad, and I want you to love me. I'm angry at you, Dad, and I need you to hear me...

To be your son has meant many things to me. It means that there is a profound bond that exists between us that defies the differences that any two people naturally share. It means that you have shared with me part of your spirit, your vision, and your concern for our small planet and the billions of people that inhabit it. And it also means that we are two people who, with our individual and mutual skills and resources and knowledge, can help each other to achieve the happiness and satisfaction in our own lives that is essential to bringing it into the lives of others. We have so much to give to each other. Together we are a formidable team.

I feel the pain of the young husband and father who wrote those words. He was a first-generation farmer, with strong political ideals and a belief that the world could be changed at the level of the soil. He believed Robert McNamara was his partner in this.

There was an imbalance. My father was too silent on the most important subjects in our lives. In that letter, I think I let him win again. We could be father and son, we could be partners, we could be two men with the name McNamara. But we couldn't really be a team. I know I'm yearning for something that might not have been possible. Wanting an unattainable thing leads to dark thoughts. It leads me to bitterness, to vehemence.

It may not have been so bad. It may just be that we lacked the depth of language and the emotional clarity to integrate the two compartments of our lives—love and strife—into a more holistic pattern. I doubt whether many fathers and sons arrive at such understanding.

In letters to his friends, which I have in my farm office, my father sometimes refers to "Craig's dream to save the world through farming." He's not wrong to call it that; yet I sense a certain sarcasm there that is hurtful. As a farmer, I've been hardworking, ambitious, and strategic. These were all qualities that Dad passed on to me, but I'm not sure what he ultimately thought about my career choices.

In "The Road Not Taken," one of my father's favorite poems by Robert Frost, Frost concludes:

Two roads diverged in a wood, and I—
I took the one less traveled by,
And that has made all the difference.

We chose different roads. I would like to think that I chose a more honest one. I know that I tried to bury a lot of guilt in the soil. Dad lived with guilt in silence, in a Washington office. The distance between our paths reflects an absence in our relationship. It was not just physical; the lack of honesty was even greater.

Then again, this poem is not really about the importance of the two paths. It's about the folly of constructing neat narratives and explanations in retrospect.

5.

The Chipper Gene

Dad arrived home after fourteen-hour workdays. When I heard him come through the door, I bolted down the stairs from my bedroom, gave him a big hug, and began my litany of the day's highlights. We'd be sitting in the Green Room, Dad on the brocade couch, his suit rumpled. I sat hopefully on a Harvard chair in front of him. Earlier, before he got home, I enjoyed fantasies of being a grown-up in the Green Room. There was a Steuben sculpture of Excalibur in there, in two pieces. I loved pulling the silver sword out of its crystal stone.

Dad liked scotch on the rocks. While he sat on the couch with his drink, he would rest his left hand on a small black-walnut block, topped with his silver calendar. The calendar was engraved with the dates of the Cuban Missile Crisis, the Thirteen Days. It also bore his initials, RSM, and those of the president, JFK. This calendar had been a gift from Jackie Kennedy.

While Dad was sipping his drink, I recounted my seventh-grade football game from the afternoon. I had a big run right up the middle of the field, splitting defenders, cruising toward the end zone. His eyes faded a little, while his fingers traced the calendar. I realized that he was not listening to my story. He was remembering, silently, the days of the crisis. He wore a still expression. He was being hollowed out. Gazing up into that distant face, I started to think, *Is it time to get out of the room?*

When his ice clinked, or his hand moved back to his lap, our conversation resumed its rhythm. He coughed. It had been a blip. I kept babbling.

This is my strongest memory of the Cuban Missile Crisis. The one object, the silver calendar, after the fact. In October of 1962 I had no idea that Dad was going to work every day feeling afraid of not coming home. My parents did an amazing job of buffering. I don't even remember going to church, as many people did during that time. Mom and Dad's protection of me was so total, so complete. I remember visiting the home of Dad's deputy secretary of defense, Roswell Gilpatric, on the Maryland shore. They had an underground shelter, and our families got to go down there to explore. Climbing down the ladder in my cowboy boots and ducking my head into the darkness, I thought it was an adventure.

My mother and father were my bomb shelter, more than any bunker. I enjoyed the particular attention given to the youngest child in the family. Free days with Mom and Dad were the highlights of my childhood. Some of my best memories involve riding in the family Ford from Ann Arbor to the sandy shores of Lake Michigan near Old Mission. Sometimes, on a very long drive, I'd rub Dad's sore back. In the winters we always went skiing. After a long day on the slopes, there would be back rubs all around.

Long before we used sunscreen and ChapStick to prevent sun damage, my lips cracked during those sultry hot summers and bright snowy winters. And of course I would lick them because they hurt, and this created a large red circle of soreness from my nose to my chin. My mother lovingly referred to me as Happy, because I looked like a clown, but also because I had a predilection for being happy.

My family has something called the "chipper gene." My wife coined this term after I had lived for years without knowing the diagnosis. The chipper gene is a way of getting by, and also a bit of a curse. Sometimes I don't even notice myself being chipper, the way you don't notice your own hand gestures.

One of my father's favorite catchphrases was "It's a glorious day!" That expression summarizes the whole idea of the chipper gene. He would say "It's a glorious day" constantly, regardless of what kind of day it was. The sentiment survived all the changes in our relationship. When my daughter, Emily, was just five or six years old, she picked up on it. She would parrot Dad by saying, "It's a glorious day, sweetie!" She'd lower her voice and puff out her cheeks, her eyes taking in the grins of all within earshot.

Glorious days come every so often, not every day. I started to realize this in my midtwenties and thirties, when I began to address my own mental health through counseling. Meanwhile, I think Dad's mental health deteriorated starting in his sixties. As I observed him over the last decades of his life, I realized that his glorious days were few and far between.

I remember one instance when we were at the Watergate hotel restaurant together. Out of the various dinners we had, this one stands out. It was after my mother's death, and Dad had been living in an apartment in the Watergate for a few years, having moved out of the Tracy Place house. I felt happy to be with him, but when we sat down at the table, he seemed immediately agitated. He was coughing a lot, a symptom of diverticulitis of the esophagus, which he struggled with throughout his later years.

The server greeted him politely, but Dad rushed him.

"Sir! Two chardonnays."

As we waited, he kept trying to get the server's attention. "Sir! Sir!" He wanted to know when the wine was going to show up. I talked to him about farming, and I tried to lead him to a question about my children. It didn't work. When the wine came, he finally started to relax.

I can recall the shape of a bending ski track. The redness of his cheek on a winter's day. I remember certain patches of wildflowers, where they grew, and trailside lunches. I remember eating walnuts on hikes and ski trips, carrying them for him—their weight in my bag. Why, then, in remembering that dinner, a time when I know I witnessed him in such quiet, restrained agony, do I have to search my memories? I recall the simple and pleasant things about the restaurant. The white tablecloths, a view of the Potomac. What he said, how he treated me, and what we did afterward—these things I don't remember very well.

The need for my days to be glorious has impeded memory. And it impeded understanding for decades of my life, the critical ones when we were both men, equals, not just father and son.

My father's Cuban Missile Crisis calendar, a gift from Jackie Kennedy in 1963

Nowadays, the notion that every day is glorious seems like an inflexible expectation. We had many of those in my family. There were several innocuous yet unbreakable rules: no gum chewing, tuck in your shirt, never say damn, look people in the eye, be a good Scout, don't tell lies, wake up early, no need for a bathrobe, don't join country clubs, golf is a waste of time, work hard, never quit. That last one was literally the opposite of what we needed to do in Vietnam.

There were also more complex expectations. I think Dad expected me to understand and accept him, even when his complexity crossed the line into hypocrisy.

I remember one conversation we had about right and wrong. This was in the mid-1980s. Following my mother's death, Dad had retired from the World Bank and begun a new career that consisted of serving on numerous boards and writing books. At that time I still viewed him as a basically decent person with occasional bad judgment. I can't remember where we were for the talk, but it was probably a camping trip. We were probably drinking a can of sweet red wine. I raised a question about hard choices.

"Gray is everywhere," my father said. "Especially when we think that we know the truth."

"You really feel that way?" I asked. It had never seemed so. Not in our house, not in our relationship. I had always thought that things were clear to him. The rules had been clear, his love for me had been clear. The gloriousness of life had been clear.

Perhaps I poked at it again. "I never thought of that, Dad. What do you mean?"

The conversation ended haltingly. We got into our sleeping bags and lay on the ground under the open night sky. I anticipated waking up in the morning and shaking the dew off my bag, and I hoped Dad would say something to shake away all the lies between us, everything that had created such an absence of understanding. He soon fell asleep, without saying the word *Vietnam*, having said no more than what he intended. I watched the stars, which in the moments before sleep stood out as very white against a sheet of black.

On my desk sits a Buddha. It's carved from rosewood, a deep red-brown. I like to think that many hands have held and polished it.

A small infant climbs on the Buddha's warm, round belly. The infant's eyes are wide, gazing up in an adoring and joyful expression. The babe's mouth is open as if in the middle of a gurgling laugh. The Buddha's mouth, lined with ivory teeth, returns the laugh.

This Buddha was my father's. It sat on his desk in our Washington home. To the best of my knowledge, he bought it in China. During World War II, he had served in the US Army Air Forces Office of Statistical Control. He was deployed to India, where he used his statistical skills to organize the transportation of fuel and cargo. He was also responsible for analyzing bombing operations to make them more efficient. Dad only ever told me one story about this period of his life, his actual military service. One day he flew a B-29 mission over the Hump, the eastern end of the Himalayas, and landed on an airstrip in China. As he peered from the bomber's window, he saw hundreds of Chinese peasants pulling a stone roller the size of a small house, attempting to smooth the rough surface of the landing strip. In an instant, a worker tripped and was crushed to death as the stone roller ran over him. The Buddha in my office, to the best of my knowledge, was purchased during that trip.

I wonder what that Buddha meant to Dad. Did Dad see himself in the omnipotence of the Buddha's great, smooth head? Did he feel the joy of the infant climbing the curves of the Buddha's belly, possibly wondering if this would be his experience with his own son? I wonder why that story from his brief time in China—briefly miraculous, suddenly tragic—was the only one he told me.

Buddhism teaches us that life is full of suffering. Only by

accepting this fact can we begin practices that will alleviate our suffering. This is the opposite of denial. I look at the small, polished figure on my desk and think that the Buddha would laugh at hearing an expression like "It's a glorious day" uttered during days of war and sickness.

6.

Firefall

Starting before I was ten years old, we went on summer packing trips across the California Sierras. Our usual route began in Reds Meadows, on the eastern slopes, and took us over the range. On each trip, we got to climb peaks that went into the clouds. We'd go skinny-dipping in the frigid alpine lakes above the tree line. At night, the stars were audience to our tall tales around the fire, stories of the enormous fish we'd caught and the treacherous mountains we'd climbed, and the light danced over us.

These Sierra trips brought together some of my parents' closest friends from the Cal Berkeley circle. I remember trips with the Haas family, the Goodins, and the Goodwins. We were the Macs. The other families also had three kids each, with boys my age and daughters my sisters' age. We all enjoyed the excitement of being in nature with equals, a deep sense of community while getting away from the city.

With so many people in our party, we'd hire an outfitter and saddle up mule teams of fifteen animals to pack in our gear and food. Accompanied by the wranglers, cooks, and cowboys, we'd sometimes have a party of twenty-five or thirty hikers out there in the wilderness.

A pack train is a lovely sight to look upon. Cowboys guide the sure-footed mules over every type of terrain. Each mule bears two neatly packed loads, one on each side, and the packs wobble as the animals step, forming a row of living symmetrical movement. If it's a dry and dusty trail, you can see a great big cloud kicked up behind the party. It all feels very nostalgic, evoking images of the frontier. The mornings would begin with an amazing breakfast and a whole lineup of lunch items. On top of long granite boulders, the outfitters would lay tins of kipper snacks and Ritz crackers, bread, ham, and olives. I enjoyed going through the line and making lunch with my sisters, which made me feel very self-reliant. During the day's hiking, we would all be on the trail together. In the evening, after camp was set up, the parents would go on short walks with cups of wine.

Those times were rich and colorful, filled with excitement. We weren't a particularly religious family, and I always felt that the mountains were our cathedral. I got to see my parents at their best on those pack trips. Dad was able to take in deep breaths of pure air and measure himself not in production statistics or numerical reports from the field of war but in miles hiked.

I remember one site where we stayed, at Mirror Lake. I was so excited to set up camp. As the grown-ups pitched tents and put together their fly rods to fish, my good friend Sandy and I threw down our tent and sleeping bags in a gentle swale, just perfect to protect us from the evening breeze and allow us a good view of the stars. We figured we would set up the tent when we got back. Then we headed down to the lake with our rods and tackle, ready to catch the Big Ones that we had heard swam in those waters.

While we were fishing, an evening storm cracked and rolled in over the pass. By the time we returned to our camping spot, our tent and sleeping bags were floating. The swale had filled with rain. It was quite a task to fish everything out. I imagine that some of the adults were angry with us, while others were worried. Perhaps the wranglers and cowboys, who had been doing this sort of thing dozens of times every summer for their whole lives, had a laugh about it. In the end, we dried things out by the fire, and that night we slept underneath the stars, listening to the sounds of the horses breathing and the quiet ring of the bells around the mules' necks. In the sunshine of the morning we laid our wet gear on the dewy grass and let the rising heat cook off the dampness and condensation. Lesson learned: be more careful. It was a blissful education.

Gathering firewood at camp was another adventure. To a kid, it wasn't work; it was pure fun. There were lots of freshly fallen pine branches around. You wanted to gather all the various sizes of wood—from the tiniest dry twigs for igniting the campfire to the most gigantic logs, which would burn for hours. Sandy and I, being young boys, were of course more focused on turning this sensible task into a contest of strength. We liked to see who could drag the biggest log back to camp. We'd daringly snap the large, skinny ones in half, making the peeling bark fly into the air and into our faces. We'd keep piling kindling into our arms until sticks were falling from the sides of our bundles.

The largest logs required the most skill. On one occasion, I was maneuvering a gorgeous log across a fallen ponderosa pine. Somehow, a half-broken branch got stuck under the tree trunk. Trying to yank it up, I pulled too hard and took a fall and managed to put a significant gash in my scalp. With no medical facility within several days of camp, Will Goodwin, a UCLA-trained urologist, stitched me up right then and there with a needle and fishing line. I can't remember whether I was in shock, crying hysterically as a kid might, or gritting my teeth to impress Sandy and the adults.

After gathering fuel came the best part of all: starting the fire. At the crest of evening, when the sun started to fall, the sparks got going. Sometimes the cowboys started it, and sometimes it was my father. After all the hard work of hiking or riding, fishing or swimming, and dragging wood around, this process was like reaping the fruits of our labor, and it taught me to savor the pleasure of coming to the end of a day. When real darkness set in, we'd circle the fire, jostling for a good spot away from the direction of the smoke, and when we were all settled, I'd look at each face, everyone in my family and in the other families. I remember the light of the fire, singing together, and the joy of being together in nature.

These are only some of many wilderness memories I have. Incredible experiences all. Even the minor dangers that come from being so long in the wilderness, and the small instances of violence—gutting a fish, injuring myself—were natural to that temporary mountain existence. I remember glissading down steep snowfields in the radiant sun, picking up speed and hurtling toward a broad field at the bottom, a little out of control and yet confident and assured of a successful landing. There were treacherous trails that made my heartbeat accelerate, and I remember the relief of summiting a pass and catching my breath.

On one pack trip in 1961, we guided our horses up to Little Pothole Lake. The trail goes through forest and alpine tundra, and it's four miles up to the Kearsarge Pass at 11,700 feet. The path was narrow, and our steps sometimes sent rocks and small boulders hurtling down the slopes. A month before we made the pass, a team of mules on the same crossing had fallen to their death. Broken and twisted by packing twine and rope and by the brutal fall, this unfortunate mule train was strangled, almost hung, on either side of a huge boulder. The only way that the Forest Service could remove them from the face of the granite pass was to dynamite their corpses, leaving a blast radius of body parts. Down the slope, we saw heads peeking out from boulders, hooves dangling like clothes hangers, and huge mule haunches with the tails still intact, all positioned like furniture on the side of the trail.

I didn't think of it as violent, and I wasn't afraid. The blood was dry and far away. I saw in those body parts a process of nature. They would decay. Taking part in the religion of the mountains, I felt myself in touch with the cycle of death and regeneration.

We did a Sierra trip almost every year in the early 1960s, and they continued into the mid-'60s. As the young kids got older, we started carrying backpacks and went without mules. These were true celebrations of nature. Nobody criticized my father or accused him of lying. The conversation among the adults was lively and rich. They sang folk songs around the campfire. "You Are My Sunshine" was one of the songs they liked to sing.

We would end up at the Ahwahnee Hotel, on the western side of the Sierras. Knowing that the secretary of defense was arriving, the management at the hotel always reserved the presidential suite for my parents. There, they relaxed at the end of a long hike. The room had views of the Firefall, a Yosemite Valley ritual in which a neighboring hotel's owners pushed burning embers off the side of a cliff, creating a spectacular light show.

One of our later backpacking trips took place in 1965, a few months after the start of Operation Rolling Thunder. The US bombing campaign, which my father later admitted was a misguided strategy with unconscionable costs in civilian lives, had begun in March. I remember that particular trip because we ran into a park ranger on the second or third day of the trek. I first noticed him following us at a distance. Later, he caught up with us when we were stopping to rest on the trail. Nobody acknowledged him. We continued along, and he lingered behind to give us a little distance and privacy. I understood that he was there as security for my father. In an emergency, this ranger was responsible for getting Robert McNamara safely off the mountain. Neither Dad nor Mom mentioned it. They had always tried to keep me from noticing security forces. By that time, when I was fifteen, this was becoming impossible, because my own powers of observation had grown.

If I knew then what I know now, I might have brought up the war around the campfire. I might have said, "Dad, how can you be out here while that's going on?" Or maybe I would have fallen back with the ranger, made a new friend, and told him my true feelings. That didn't happen; I still didn't know enough. I didn't know that across the Pacific Ocean, at the same time that my mother and I were casting our fishing lines, thousands of Vietnamese women and boys were shouldering vehicle parts, ammunition, and other supplies down the Ho Chi Minh trail. Our lack of vehicles and our exposure to the elements on this trip made for a pleasant diversion. Meanwhile, other human beings were braving heat and storms on foot to follow mountain and jungle roads into battle, with American bombs falling on them as the US Empire attempted to slow and disrupt their movement along the trail.

It's likely that by 1966, the last year we did a Sierra trek as a family, there were bombs dropping and exploding at the very same moment that my mother and father were enjoying the sights of the Firefall from their suite in the Ahwahnee. It haunts and brutalizes my dreams, knowing this. I have been removed only by one degree of responsibility from unnatural violence.

The Colorado Rockies were my family's true mountain home. Aspen, in particular, called to my parents. They had first visited in the 1950s, those peaceful years, and I'm sure that in their minds, Aspen retained a sort of innocence even into the '60s.

It was a bit less developed back then, a bit more isolated. Around Aspen, my mother and father watched the alpine glow from many vistas: camping spots, highway pullouts, and peaks at the end of hiking trails. Together, they skied the back slopes of the Rockies. In these situations, they could disappear from public life. It made sense that, during the darkest days of the war, Dad would find solace there.

One summer day in 1967, everything changed. I was seventeen. My understanding of the war was now fairly substantial, absorbed from boarding school peers and the endless news of protests on TV and in newspapers. My parents had rented a house in Aspen for a week in order to oversee the construction of a new home they were building in Snowmass. One afternoon, as we were returning from a hike up to Cathedral Lake, a large group of local antiwar activists showed up to picket our place. More specifically, they were there to confront my father.

The meadow in which the protesters stood was covered with Colorado columbines and Indian paintbrush. Wheatgrass swayed in the afternoon breeze, creating a lazy feel. It was one of the calmest settings for a protest that you could imagine.

Mom and Dad quickly entered the house, dodging the protesters on their way in. I think they were worried about their safety. Antiwar demonstrations across the country had often turned violent, and here they were, on vacation, without any security.

The door shut, but it didn't lock. I decided to remain outside. I wanted to meet everyone and talk with them. This was not defiance so much as my natural instinct.

I think that the protesters did most of the talking. I remember that their words were even and kind. I remember how their long braids and beards glistened in the sunlight of midafternoon. There weren't any profane chants or accusatory slogans; they were persuasive and eloquent. In contrast, the tone of my voice, every word I spoke, was blighted with embarrassment. My throat shook a little. The man they had come to speak with was not there beside me, standing in the meadow. I don't know what Dad was feeling. I can only guess it was some combination of anger, fear, flight, sadness, and remorse. I know what I was feeling: abandoned and alone.

I will never forget the handmade peace placards that the protesters carried. Thomas Benton, a well-known local artist, had designed them. They projected the sincerity of the protesters' belief that the war was wrong, that we should end it. The posters came from nearby, made with materials and by an artist from within this small community; the peace movement was coming from the ground up. To the protesters, it surely seemed that men like Robert McNamara were mere visitors in Aspen, Washington bureaucrats imperiously wrecking our country from the top down—from industrial heights—and then parachuting into the mountains for a vacation.

Before the protesters walked back across that meadow, they gave me one of the posters. For years it hung on my bedroom wall. To the best of my memory, my parents and I didn't even talk about the protest after I said farewell to my new friends and went back inside. I took a shower, washing off the dried sweat from our long hike, and proceeded to have dinner like any other night. Looking back now, I see how wholly I had absorbed my father's unwillingness to talk about the war. It didn't even occur to me to ask him to acknowledge what had just happened outside. I knew that he would just get quiet if I pressed him.

I was becoming one of the people in the meadow. The feeling I had was solidarity with them. The protesters were there to talk to my father about the war, and he had ignored them in much the same way that he ignored me. The inspiration of that evening still grows wild in my heart, like the paintbrushes in the meadow. But the memories are wilted and picked over. I'm not exactly sure what I was thinking at that moment, when I turned my back on my parents and stayed outside. It felt natural, almost accidental, because intrinsically I knew the war was wrong. I couldn't push against my own heart.

This poster, designed by the artist Thomas Benton, was given to me by the protesters who came to the door of my family's home in Aspen in 1967.

PART 2

7.

Army

My St. Paul's grades had not been good. Probably Dad's name contributed to my admission to Stanford. My older sister Margy had attended before me, and it felt right to follow in her footsteps, but the greatest factor in my college decision was the desire to escape Washington, New England, and the entire East Coast.

It was 1969 in the Bay Area, and I was nineteen. This was a new world, and I was a boy, trying to become a man. Some of my boarding school peers were coming with me. Still, Palo Alto was vastly different from anywhere I'd lived. At St. Paul's, I'd first begun to be tormented by my father's role in the history of the twentieth century. Now I was in the land of my demons, and the demons were all real. Northern California was the home of hippies and a stronghold of antiwar activism. The evils of the war were not swirling in the back of my mind; they were being shouted in the street.

Like it is for any young man entering adulthood, it was my destiny to confront the legacy of my father. Dad was now the subject of both public admiration (by those already nostalgic for the Kennedy era) and public pillorying (by both radicals and Republicans). His refusal to speak publicly and to pressure his successors to get out of Vietnam was a primary reason that I started to protest the war. If he wouldn't tell the truth, I would do it for him. At the time, I thought I was taking control of my own life. Really, I was carrying some of his weight.

It would have been odd to remain silent. Dissent against the war was no longer underground, if it had ever been. Maybe it was just easier after 1968, when Nixon was President. I no longer felt conflicted by personal attachment to the men in charge. My childhood memories no longer stood directly in the way of my anger. Richard Nixon and Henry Kissinger definitely weren't inviting me over for lunch and a swim.

There's one protest I remember very well. It must have been the autumn of 1969, my freshman year. I drove from Palo Alto to Berkeley to participate in a demonstration. I'm not sure how I heard about the event; in those days it seemed as though word traveled easily. I was going to the East Bay, and I had no idea what to expect when I got there. Zooming over the water, still and silent below, I felt my anticipation growing. If you looked at me from the window of another car, you wouldn't have guessed that I was making my way into a churning pool of anguish and anger.

In Berkeley, the demonstrators gathered on one of the big central streets, lined with shops and businesses. I remember a crowd of thousands. More joined in as the cheering and chanting began. There was a staging area, hastily assembled, and I remember being somewhere toward the back of the crowd, a watcher.

The voices of the organizers boomed over speakers and echoed through the alleys. They were holding a mock trial for President Nixon, presenting the evidence for his crimes in Vietnam and his extension of the war into Cambodia. Predictably and theatrically, they found Nixon guilty. The verdict whipped the crowd into a frenzy. Soon I was running the streets, with the lights of police cars flashing around me, the scream of tires and the sound of breaking glass filling my ears. Shop windows were smashed, signs torn down, and fights started. The demonstration turned into a riot.

At first I was trying to calm people down. I remember shouting, "Don't break the windows!" I think I remember pleading logically with someone my own age, trying to convince him that the Establishment would use this destruction to paint us as violent, to portray us as hypocrites.

I'm not sure how I eventually fell into the rage. Taken up in the anger of the crowd and moved to blind emotion by the truth of our cause, I broke things and smashed glass. I talked my way out of getting arrested. I'm not quite sure how I got back to campus that night, nor how many cuts I washed out in the shower.

I was participating in the antiwar movement in order to survive my own family trauma. This template of protest was the only thing available to make sense of the ugliness in my inner world. I was unable to articulate my own chaotic feelings, but the nation presented them for me. In the streets of America I was finding a truth that provided both relief and more pain.

It wasn't all happening on the street. Back on campus, our education had become practical. We occupied administration buildings and held weekly sit-ins. In those settings, the rage simmered. One of the most important and upsetting incidents involved my literature professor. Bruce Franklin was a great teacher, a Melville expert and an articulate lecturer. I took several of his courses, and eventually the classes departed from *Moby-Dick* and focused on what was going on around us. He'd teach us to write by asking us to compose antiwar leaflets. In class discussions, we'd debate the best way to get our message out to the public. Sometimes Bruce even canceled class so we could focus on demonstrations instead.

As I recall, the entire campus was quite frequently shut down. School seemed much less important than activism. But the Establishment found ways to win. Bruce, a tenured professor, was unceremoniously canned and turned into a scapegoat. Looking back, I don't find it surprising that I dropped out after five quarters. What was I going to learn in that bubble that I couldn't see for myself in the real world? Writing my own leaflets, I wasn't the young kid who sheltered in a phone booth anymore, meekly asking his dad to send war propaganda in the mail.

There was one time during this period, which was usually full of tremendous energy, when I got a preview of the quiet, burning sadness I would feel in years to come. It was during a protest at the San Francisco Airport. A few of us occupied one of the main terminal buildings.

The terminal was extremely crowded that day. We stood in the middle of the big marble floor and read aloud the names of US soldiers killed in Vietnam. The stack of papers with the list of names was enormous, so we'd take turns. One person would read for a few hours, and then the next person would take over.

The majority of people in the airport ignored us. A few of them probably nodded or waved in support. The thing I remember most is the few men—all of them men, most in their fifties—who tried to threaten and intimidate us. They called us sons of bitches and worse. The name-calling didn't really hurt. It stung me more when someone yelled, "You haven't been there."

This insult brought to mind all my childhood memories. I hated thinking about those fifteen-odd years when I had been relatively clueless about the war. Adding to a kind of survivor's guilt, I now also suffered from impostor syndrome. *You haven't been there* hurt because it was true. I didn't know very much. I certainly didn't know anything about the people we were fighting in Vietnam.

Hearing those men scream at us in the airport—knowing that a few of them were probably World War II veterans—made me think of rubbing Dad's back in the ski lodge and seeing him listen to the words of the Quakers. I felt now that I should have been standing shoulder to shoulder with those people, facing him and confronting him. As a child I couldn't imagine that my father would do something he knew was wrong. It had taken me too long to see the truth.

In the years after I became involved in the peace movement, *You haven't been there* turned into *You weren't there*. Because I wasn't. I didn't go.

When I was at Stanford, I had the opportunity to take a deferment. So did my peers. We were college kids, and therefore the Establishment valued our lives. Many of us were the sons of Establishment leaders.

I had learned from other activists that deferments were both racist and classist. On a personal level, I thought taking a deferment amounted to going along with the war planners, taking my father's side. By 1969, my father was no longer at the Pentagon. Still, I figured that he must have approved the use of deferments while he was in office, or at least had allowed them to continue.

I don't remember the process involved in refusing the deferment—whether I had to actively decline one or if I simply didn't request one. My memory really kicks in when I received my draft notice at Donner House on the Stanford campus. After getting the summons, I took a bus from San Jose to the nearest induction center. It was a long ride around the Bay to Oakland. I remember that I was on a Greyhound bus. It was hot, and the seats were filled. I felt a sense of approaching doom, like being pursued by a figure of Death in a dream.

At the gates of the induction center, there were antiwar protesters handing out pamphlets urging us to resist. Chanting, singing songs. Of course, most of the draftees weren't from Stanford. There were kids from all the surrounding communities, and they were of every race. Still, I remember that the majority of kids had brown skin; the inequities of the draft were obvious. Some of the protesters came up to us as we stood in line to inform us about all the different ways that we could get classified 4-F, ineligible for service. The message was *You don't have to do this.*

The draft board treated us like cattle. Once inside, we were poked and prodded. The main part of the day consisted of a humiliating physical. We were stripped and searched, for the contraband of weakness. It felt like they were denuding us mentally too.

The last inspection was with a shrink. This guy had longish

hair and a thick beard. He asked me if there were any psychological reasons why I couldn't serve in the military, and he asked in such a sincere way. I was honest with him. I told him that I was completely against the war. Maybe I mentioned going to a Quaker school. He seemed to hear me. Surely this was someone who understood that I was a tormented soul.

"Anything else?"

It was almost like he wanted me to make something up. Like he was saying, *This is your chance.* I'd heard stories of the things people would say to the army shrinks. One friend of mine even lied about his sexuality and told them he was gay.

I didn't make up any stories that day. Unless—and this seems truer in retrospect—every story I told about myself back then was partially made up, partially constructed from conflicting desires. To serve, to not die. To be a good soldier, to be true to myself. That day, the only story I told was one that felt very true: I told the shrink that I had stomach ulcers. That was my medical issue.

With his hair and beard, the psychologist had made himself look almost like a hippie. He was attentive and sensitive as a listener when I told him about the ulcers. He asked me how long I had been experiencing them. He asked me to describe my symptoms. I breathed easier, sensing the decision would be made for me—they would not send me.

"Have you been to a doctor?"

Yes, I told him. The conversation ended shortly after that. The shrink said I was good to go. He waved me through, a 1-A. I was good to fight.

After my visit to the draft board, probably just a few days later, my brother-in-law helped me contact the doctor who had diagnosed me with ulcers. I don't remember if I took the initiative in this, or if the draft board requested documentation as a result of my statements to the psychologist. Whatever the case, the doc ultimately wrote a letter confirming that he'd been treating my ulcers for years. Finally, on December 19, 1969, I got a notice in the mail, addressed to my dorm room, informing me that I was "medically disqualified under current medical fitness standards for induction into the Armed Forces."

I wasn't allowed to serve. I say *allowed* because it's a true word. I had conflicted feelings all along, and I have them still, but one thing is clear: not going to Vietnam as a soldier still causes me overwhelming guilt. It's like a gap in my soul. On some level, I believed that serving would pay a debt for my father's involvement in the war. To whom, I'm not sure. Maybe to humanity, maybe to some disembodied spirit of justice, maybe to our relationship, as a form of communication in place of what had not been said out loud. I didn't want military glory. I certainly didn't want to kill anyone. I didn't believe in the cause. I just felt that I had this obligation, which I didn't fulfill.

I always thought it was ironic that ulcers were the thing that got me out of serving. I believed they were caused by the stress I felt throughout the mid-1960s, attributable to my boarding school struggles and my dysfunctional relationship with Dad. Did Dad ever think about this? Did he even consider it? Maybe he would be relieved to know that he caused me so much anxiety that I was 4-F, safe and sound. Is it even a good thing to be safe when you're living with that level of physical stress?

The ulcers shouldn't have been disqualifying. They didn't

disqualify me from backpacking in the Sierras and skiing in Colorado. In recent years I've come to understand more about the bacterial origins of ulcers, and I am less certain that they were directly attributable to my particular childhood traumas.

Would fighting in a bad war have made any of this better? Would it have made my life easier to live—if I had survived—in the aftermath? Would it have improved my relationship with my father? I doubt it, but the guilt and regret are still there, feeding off the possibilities.

There were plenty of draftees who had some sort of medical issue but couldn't afford medical visits. Others didn't have relatives willing to help them navigate the process. There were also young men who wanted to go—some too young to serve, some too skinny or too sickly—who did everything in their power to make sure that they got over there, out of a sense of duty. I wasn't that person.

I feel certain that my father did not intervene in this matter. I never talked to him about it, so my belief is unconfirmed, but it probably doesn't make a difference that it's unconfirmed. If I had spoken to him, there's no possibility that he would have told me the truth. I'm certain that if I had asked, "Dad, did you get me 4-F'ed?" he would have fallen silent. He didn't even have anything to say about my decision to show up at the induction.

He was out of government in 1969, then serving as the president of the World Bank, and this fact adds to my belief that he didn't pull any strings. It was probably the lowest point in our relationship, when I dissociated from him the most and he understood me the least.

Reflecting on my draft experience now, trying to understand, feeling both enormous guilt and gratitude for being alive, I see myself in the year 1969 as a person with only partial agency, swept along by this complicated history. In other words, I was a kid. The son of Robert McNamara but a kid all the same. This all happened during my first three months on the Stanford campus. The ones who went were kids too.

Last year, as we were in the midst of the walnut harvest, I met a Vietnam veteran. He was one of the truck drivers who arrived at the farm every morning to load our product and transport it to wholesalers. As I greeted him, and we waited for the out-loading conveyor belt to do its work, he told me a little about his life. It turned out that he was born in 1950, the same year as me. He went to a rural high school in Northern California. After he graduated, he said, there were no opportunities. So he enlisted.

"Are you glad you did that?" I asked. I didn't know what else to say.

"It was the worst and the best decision of my life," the truck driver told me.

I asked him what he meant by that.

"The worst decision was going."

And the best decision, he explained, was the time when he refused to follow orders. A superior had commanded him to destroy a hamlet where it was suspected that some of the villagers were sheltering VCs. He didn't do it. He stood down.

I didn't ask the driver what happened next. He didn't say whether or how he was punished for his insubordinate act. If he had followed orders, I suppose his punishment would have been to live with the knowledge that he had destroyed innocent lives. That knowledge would still be with him, even in the moment when we stood in the early-morning dark together.

While the truck driver told me his story, I listened. I didn't say a word. The guy had no clue whose son I was. He drove off, and the sun was coming up, and I faded away from that conversation about Vietnam, which I've been having my whole adult life. It stops and starts, and it happens with different people and at different times. For me it is one ongoing confession. I went back to my land that morning, back into the harvest and the soil.

8.

Going Down the Road, Feeling Bad

After the Army turned me down, things at Stanford got dark. My assigned roommate was as conservative as the Confederate Army, so even the place where I slept was uncomfortable. I was spending more time protesting the war than going to class, but our protests weren't stopping the violence. It was a frustrating cycle: protest, smash a window, rinse, repeat. By now I knew a lot about the stalemate in Vietnam: the increased troop deployments, the rising casualties, the certainty of defeat. My understanding of the situation had evolved to the point where I felt rage at my father. This was still before the leaking of the Pentagon Papers, which publicly confirmed his long-held private skepticism about the war and his dishonesty. But I realized that he must have known, all along, that we couldn't win.

I felt like a draft dodger at the time, though I don't put myself in that category now. To cope with my shame, I drank and smoked dope. At one point, I sold a small bag of cocaine to a friend who got caught with it in the airport when returning from an overseas trip. He had to hire a good DC lawyer in order to get off. I found out about this years later, and the incident clarified the feeling I remember from back then, the sense that everything I touched caught on fire. Yet I was never the primary victim, never the one who got burned. I only felt guilt and embarrassment and insecurity. What was I doing with myself?

Whatever waited after graduation was unappealing. Getting a job, moving to suburbia, and starting a nuclear family seemed like going along with the Establishment. There was talk in the streets and in class of radical new lifestyles: communes, traveling circuses, free love. People my age were leaving the country to do things like join the Venceremos Brigade, an organization of American students who traveled to Cuba to work on farms and support revolution. Was I even going to graduate from college with the grades I had? I'd enjoyed some literature classes at Stanford, and I wrote some poetry, but I had no idea what I wanted to do after college. I only had a strong sense that it needed to be far removed from Washington, DC, politics, business, and the military-industrial complex.

So when my friend Will suggested we travel to the southernmost tip of South America in the spring of 1971, I didn't need much persuading.

I met Will at St. Paul's. He was the friend I wanted to be: tall, handsome, and a talented performer. He seemed so self-assured, so confident. At prep school we'd starred together in a production of *Julius Caesar*. Will was Brutus, and I was Caesar, and I remember his performance being almost as good as James Mason's. I'm sure he must have carried my weight, and he probably helped me rehearse my lines. To this day, I have no idea how I ever succeeded in memorizing lines like "But I am constant as the Northern Star, / of whose true-fixed and resting quality / there is no fellow in the firmament." And I'll never forget Will's delivery of some of Brutus's responses. "O Rome, I make thee promise. If the redress will follow, thou receivest / thy full petition at the hand of Brutus."

Will went on to perform in many other plays in high school and college. He starred alongside Sigourney Weaver in the Stanford production of *Androcles and the Lion*. My recollection is that I was part of the Christian mob. I was mesmerized by Sigourney, who was portraying a Christian slave. I'm guessing that the budget for the play was on the thin side, because Will wore his motorcycle helmet, decorated with pine branches in place of laurels.

He loved his motorcycle. When it came time for us to set off south, Will insisted that we really needed to do this Latin America trip on bikes. I remember having some questions. First of all, I didn't have enough money. Plus, wouldn't it be much more engaging to go by bus or hitchhiking so that we could meet people along the way?

Will was so wonderfully convincing. He meticulously described the joys of riding motorcycles through Mexico and Central America. As if giving a stage performance, he made me imagine the feeling of freedom we would get cruising south as if pulled by gravity. The performance he gave was worthy of *Easy Rider*. Just that quickly, I became a believer. Will also succeeded in recruiting our friend Rob for the trip. Rob was an East Coast kid like me. He had grown up on Long Green Farm outside Baltimore. His mother and father were, in his words, "gentlemen farmers." All his life, Rob had been raising cattle, turkeys, green beans, corn, and tomatoes. He studied mycology and (later) wine making.

I don't think any of us gave much thought to the ultimate goal of this trip. It was the middle of our sophomore year. I had been living out of the house since I was fifteen years old, first at St. Paul's and then at Stanford. I had worked the previous summer on a trail crew, and I felt completely confident in my outdoorsmanship and my competence as a traveler. At that time, I saw my parents only during vacations, most often in Colorado. Dropping out of college seemed completely natural, and I didn't think about whether I would return to school or not.

Apparently the only motorcycle to buy was a BMW 650. Will found a dealer in Redwood City. We made the journey there and bargained for some new bikes. I gave my bike the nickname Boojum, inspired by Edward Koren's illustrations of a Lewis Carroll monster. Rob's bike was named Maytag because it was white and reminded us of a Maytag washing machine. Will's was called the "Arf Train," and I'm not sure what that name meant. We made a lot of trips to assemble a hodgepodge of makeshift gear. We didn't have fairing pouches or motorcycle panniers to store our belongings in, so we had to customize carriers ourselves. We bought aluminum attachments made for airplanes, rigged them to the rear of the motorcycles, and loaded them with spare tires and parts. The wearable gear was pretty rudimentary too. We had bulky waxed cotton raincoats and pants that got stiff and hotter than hell in the steamy Costa Rican jungles. Of course Will's motorcycle monologues didn't mention that part.

We left school with a few AAA maps and no Spanish. As I remember it, we each had some cash and about $300 dollars in traveler's checks, and we assumed that would last us the duration of the trip. Will, Rob, and I rode out of Palo Alto on a bright spring day in 1971. I was leaving behind my country, a partial Stanford education, and my activism. The road ahead was uncertain. Our only goal was to get to Tierra del Fuego, but by no particular date. I was riding away from all my feelings about my father and my country, and I thought I could leave them behind.

What I would discover over the next two and a half years, winding my way from Palo Alto to Chile, was a deeper understanding of the crisis unfolding in our American democracy. I would witness firsthand things I'd seen on the news: war, racism, and imperialism. Without intention, I would discover a path to my future career, farming. I would encounter utter loneliness, kindness beyond belief, beauty, political upheaval and revolution, sickness, and transformation.

As we were departing, I wrote a poem in my journal:

Before me all my thoughts seem to reach. They look back at me and then to the sky where they take their rest. I am twenty now, I've seen twenty lives go by and I have not gone with them. I have spoken twenty words but heard no reply.
The mountains of my life have only begun...

The road south through the Sierra Madre of Monterrey was transcendent. Voluptuous waterfalls shimmered into focus among dense forests as we rounded mountain curves on our bikes.

On one of these stretches, I had my first rollover. Rounding a steep, oily uphill curve, I dumped the bike and watched as it skidded off the road. This early in the journey, we were still pretty optimistic, and my spill didn't slow us down too much. We extracted spare parts from our makeshift panniers, threw some of them on my damaged bike, and with a little ingenuity and within a few hours, I was back on the road. That night, tired and hot after the glory of a spring day in Mexico, we settled down for a meal at a roadside cantina. If you drive or take a bus through most parts of Mexico, you can still see these shady stops on the shoulders of highways, with painted concrete walls sheltering groups of simple tables, maybe protected by a tarp or canvas roof, and the smoke rising as delicious street food *antojitos* cook in big iron pots and on top of flat griddles.

Of those early weeks of the trip, I remember nothing but hospitality and warmth among the local people, despite our rudimentary language skills. We were also welcomed by plenty of mosquitoes and harsh rain. One night, after swimming in a river underneath a noisy bridge, we tried our very basic Spanish on two young Mexican guys, who assured us that the thunder, lightning, and clouds did not mean it was going to rain. After we shared a few warm beers with our new friends, the rains started up and dashed our optimism. We tried to set up a tarp for shelter to protect all our clothes and sleeping bags. Eventually, we moved under the bridge, where I cut my foot on some old glass. Rob, familiar with livestock, turned out to be the ideal companion in this situation.

He helped me wash off the cut with some boiled water and sterilized cow pies.

The problems always seemed to anticipate—if not lead to—even more problems. Once my bike was patched up, and I was patched up too, we had to endure more onslaughts. The bugs were so bad that night under the bridge that we could hardly sleep. At last we packed up, leaving at three in the morning, and drove twenty miles to a place with fewer bugs.

All the way to Mexico City we were in that early stage of travel when the joy of the open road and a kind of benign naïveté prevail. We slept just about anywhere, even in dusty fields with burros braying and roosters pecking at our packs. No one seemed to mind. And it seemed that everywhere we went, the locals took great pleasure in sharing with us their favorite meal, menudo.

Menudo is traditionally a family dish, a stew prepared with beef tripe and served on special occasions, like birthdays or Christmas. Conveniently, it's also thought to be a great cure for hangovers. It typically takes hours to prepare and is served with chopped raw onions, oregano, red chili powder, lime or lemon segments, and flour tortillas. The trick to eating menudo, if you have a gringo's stomach, is to get past the rather greasy aroma. You slurp down the pools of floating fat and entrails, then quickly stuff down tortillas to counter-balance some of the extreme bloody flavor.

I remember eating menudo at a particular roadside stop. For the nth time, we thought we were being served this delicacy because we were special guests. As the steaming bowls of beef tripe were brought before us again, we couldn't help but feel a little envious of the campesinos at the other tables, enjoying their carne asada and chili relleno. After what seemed like weeks of being served just menudo, we figured out what was happening. When waiters at the cantinas asked us what we would like to order, we always responded in broken Spanish, *"Por favor, el menu."* This was interpreted as "Menudo, please."

Near Mexico City, I took another big fall. My motorcycle tipped, and I slid a long distance on the highway. This time it wasn't only the bike that was damaged. I had a few bad scrapes, and I was lucky that I didn't snap in half. We managed to pick up the parts that had fallen off the bike. It was still roadworthy, but the alignment was affected for the rest of the trip. In our group logbook I wrote, "I know that I can't live forever, but my fall brought it too close." Looking back, I think about how many times I could have crashed. We were reckless riders. Maybe if I had died in a motorcycle crash, historians of my father's life would have written a few sentences about the irony of my death, given that so many kids died on his watch before they were twenty-one.

We arrived in Mexico City on my twenty-first birthday: April 18, 1971. We desperately needed to stop, but the city was not a restful place. I remember the haze over the cityscape as we approached, and the tint of reddish brown in the air between the buildings as we rode along streets where we saw no signs or lights. It was intimidating, and that made it feel lonely. We found La Rivera, a cheap *residencia* where we could rest awhile and keep our motorcycles parked in safety and peace. For my twenty-first birthday we bought some beers and sat around, talking and drinking a little. It was not a mood of celebration; at least I don't remember it that way.

We were regrouping and recovering. To be turning twenty-one seemed unimportant compared with our direction: south, down, away. We had been driving at a quick pace, and Mom and Dad had no idea where I was. There was no birthday phone call.

The morning after, we ventured onto the city streets to buy some food. This was when I discovered the city's fresh orange juice. It was abundant and beautiful liquid gold to me. I drank a lot of that fresh juice, like someone trying to avoid sickness, or like an invalid trying to recover. Meanwhile I picked cigarette butts off the street and sidewalk in order to have something to smoke. When I bent down, the scabs from my motorcycle crash would stretch and break open.

Calling around Mexico City to try to buy motorcycle parts, we constantly heard the words *No inglés, no inglés.* Whenever we were attempting to communicate with a local, we'd have to use unsophisticated grunts or *muchas gracias.* Sometimes we'd frustrate people to the point that they'd erupt at us in anger. Things got a little better when we met Jose. Clad in a black tie, white shirt, and black suit, he said, "Hey, *amigos.* California, *si*? You need help, no?"

Jose was about forty-five years old. His eyes moved constantly. He offered to show us Mexico City in exchange for a few cups of coffee and some tips. Somehow navigating our halting Spanish, and with very little English of his own, Jose took us to his favorite and most cherished city landmarks. One place was the Plaza de las Tres Culturas, where the Tlatelolco massacre of 1968 had occurred. Jose showed us buildings pitted by machine-gun fire, where hundreds of student demonstrators had been murdered by Mexican military police. I remember looking at the plaza and reflecting on the year 1968 in the US. In March, LBJ had announced that he would not seek reelection as president, Martin Luther King was assassinated in April, and Bobby Kennedy was gunned down weeks later. While we stood at the plaza, I remembered fleeing the St. Paul's campus to attend Bobby's burial in Arlington. Maybe that had been the first time I really woke up to the fact that something was wrong in America. The consequences for me had been limited; I was not shot, never arrested, never in danger. But there had been a quieter violence, an inner battle. I was against the war, against authority, and against my father, yet I still identified with him and was hard on myself because of the draft.

I remember standing in the plaza and feeling like an egg. My body was a shell. Somewhere at the center, there was supposed to be a yolk.

We continued with determination south from Mexico City, though our daily rate of travel varied greatly with the country's diverse terrain. One of our longest stops was in Oaxaca, the state known for its textiles and *mole*. Irregularly, we journaled and sketched in our collective logbook. We were mostly concerned about the next place to sleep—a bed or a field—and our next meal. Throughout this journey, it was possible to send letters at the *correos* and receive mail at American embassies, but there was no guarantee that our messages would reach home. More than anything else, this style of travel kept my mind from wandering too much toward the things at home that haunted me: the war, my silent father, the draft, and my uncertain future. Unlike during the vacations of my early adolescence in the American outdoors, there were no park rangers keeping tabs on us and no Quaker friends reminding us of the evils of war.

I don't remember discussing US politics with my travel buddies. As we cruised through the Yucatán, our goal was simple—to go even farther south—and the thought that we would be stopped didn't occur to me. I was fairly naive about political life outside the US. As we crossed from Mexico into Guatemala, I had no idea of the situation that was unfolding there.

When we arrived at the border crossing, an official warned us about the curfew. We couldn't travel at night, and neither could anyone else with a vehicle. The strongman in power was President Carlos Arana Osorio. Allied with death squads roaming the countryside, he was committed to pacifying Guatemala by killing the socialists who opposed him. In the 1960s, the US military had supported him in efforts to round up and kill thousands of citizens.

Bearded gringos on motorcycles (the preferred mode of transportation for guerrilla fighters) raised a minor alarm at the Guatemalan border. Young boys toting machine guns looked at us threateningly as old men sat in the shade, cutting their hair with nail clippers. I remember being frisked by some very macho military police and told we were not welcome in the country. They made us sleep on the border for two days.

Eventually, we were waved past the checkpoint. The border guards probably decided that, with our broken Spanish, we couldn't possibly understand what was going on well enough to lend aid to one side or the other. They probably figured that the danger was all ours. We rode gingerly through the verdant countryside of Guatemala, avoiding any more contact with the military police, through some of the most beautiful land I've ever laid eyes on.

When I think about what it was like to ride Boojum through Central America, all I can recall is the beauty of the landscape and an ephemeral sense of moving toward a periphery. My family and my education had been the center of my being, and this was far away from that. Guatemala was a country in a state of civil war, but I didn't really understand it until years later. Recently, I read an archived *New York Times* article from June of 1971 that describes the situation in Guatemala just as we were arriving there.

> Until mid-February, a 9 P.M.-to-5 A.M. curfew (later 11 to 5) was in force, and it could be restored at any time. In the first 12 weeks after Nov. 13 at least 1,600 persons were arrested without formal charges or arraignments, and 700 to 1,000 more—among them a dozen prominent Guatemalans—were assassinated by vigilante groups of the military and the police. Urban guerrillas with Castroite or Maoist sympathies have accounted for 25 to 30 more assassinations, mostly of army and police officers and Government informers.

Even while traveling through countries struggling with nascent democracy, civil wars, and poverty, I was never worried about safety. Probably our group didn't talk much about it. It wasn't about us, so it wouldn't affect us. We didn't know any better.

More than fear, my shadow on this journey was loneliness. I distinctly remember one moment when we were stopped somewhere in Costa Rica after a period of downtime at a gold mine owned by the father of one of our Stanford friends. I felt myself becoming depressed by the combination of dense, dark jungle and the stark economic disparity between the mine workers and owners. After we left and got back on the road, I said out loud to myself, "You have to remember. You have to remember what you're seeing in its most raw form. You have to be truthful with yourself about the complete uncertainty of life. Forty years from now, what you are experiencing today will be a story you tell about yourself. You have to remember what really happened."

The colors, customs, and flavors of Costa Rica, El Salvador, Honduras, and Nicaragua followed as we rode on through the steaming jungles and windy passes on our way to Panama. Once we got there, we were surprised to learn that the road south ended. The Pan-American Highway, a network of cobblestones and potholes, stops at the Darién Gap. To this day, there's a hundred-mile stretch of rain forest separating Central America from South America, with no passable road.

We eventually found a small fishing trawler in the port of Colón. The sailors were willing to let us come aboard. They picked our bikes up with nets and lifted them into the hold. The Arf Train, Maytag, and Boojum all rose like great mechanical marlins caught by a fisherman. We boated to San Andrés Island. From there our goal was to find a freighter to ferry us the 450 nautical miles to Cartagena, Colombia.

We spent a few weeks on San Andrés. We camped out under coconut palms, eating iguanas and sampling *ayahuasca* on that island paradise. At last we caught a freighter for our final leg to South America. I have no idea what we would have done if there hadn't been a ship willing to carry us. For now our luck held, and our group cohered.

We rode from Cartagena to Bogotá. Our motorcycles were hot and heavy after being ridden for hours through the lush green canopy of the cordillera. We had just summited a hilly overlook. Ahead lay the highway, which was really nothing more than a dirt road. I can still picture the spot: a fork in the road with a cow pasture to the left and a split-rail fence to the right. No maps, no people. This was fifty years before Google would have solved our problem instantly. Which way would we go?

I can't remember another time that I fought with Will. But on that day, Will and I had a difference of opinion. He wanted to follow the split-rail fence, and I wanted to go along the pasture. I don't remember exactly what I said. Probably it was something simple like *I'm thinking left.* Then silence. I remember the silence the most. It got very quiet as we both stewed about how correct we were. I was probably thinking of all my outdoor experiences in the Sierras, and how skilled I was at navigation. How could he not see that my instincts were good? I didn't say any of this. There was not much to talk about; it was a black-and-white choice.

At long last Will won out. His waiting game was much longer than mine. The split-rail-fence route did get us to where we needed to go: the hill town of Valdevia, just as afternoon was fading to evening. After that day, I realized that my life would always be linked to Will's. Together we've lost mothers and fathers. We've been each other's best man. I even introduced him to his wife. We didn't diverge in that moment. We became closer.

As I recall the junction, my mind goes back to my father and his favorite poem. On this journey, the fork we took did matter. On this adventure, we weren't focused on telling the stories of our lives, to ourselves or anyone else, and we weren't thinking about justifying our choices. We were just making them, surviving, and going along naturally. I remember sleeping well that night, and for many others after, even when we got to Bogotá and stayed in *pensiones* full of mosquitoes and cockroaches the size of small cats.

Finally saying goodbye to Will and Rob in Bogotá, I headed south and solo for the first time in my life. We each understood, and amicably so, that our own lives were pulling us away from one another for the time being. Rob felt the call to return home and return to school. Will remained in Bogotá and spent the next five years raising bees and selling honey in Colombia. I didn't know it at the time, but the next decade would take me along a similar path.

Devoid of company—at least, anyone who could understand English—I discovered myself in a bardo state between joy and loneliness, between a sense of discovery and a sense of being utterly lost. On that spiritual plane, with no one with whom to be in conflict, no friend or father to challenge me, experience and memory merged into one. The butterflies of the Ecuadorian jungle; working on a dairy farm in the chill of the morning, with the mist lifting off the pails of milk; hitching through the northern desert of Peru in the backs of semis carrying sugar and oil; living with a Quechua family in the highlands; making my way to Cusco in a Mini Cooper that almost fell off the mountain road; walking for four days to reach Machu Picchu.

I didn't look for these experiences. They just happened. My goal was to get to Chile, but by no particular date, and the openness of my life could be felt by the people I came across. In Ecuador I happened upon a farm where the women invited me to help them milk cows. I spent two nights on their land, sleeping on the slopes of a twenty-two-thousand-foot volcano. In the next village, I looked into the window of a small home and was invited in for five days with a mere gesture. I didn't speak a word of the language, but the man who lived there allowed me to sleep on his floor and harvest corn during the day. It's hard to remember how I communicated, but I remember that it did not feel difficult or even awkward.

There was a lonely beauty in my highland experiences. I went weeks without meeting anyone who could speak English. With Will and Rob gone, Oaxaca and Mexico City and all mail far away, a crushing loneliness overtook me on the road to Lake Titicaca. Sleeping in a pasture somewhere, I woke up to a bull staring at me, his great big animal face like something out of the depths of the darkest stage of a vision quest. Somewhere along the road, I got horribly sick and was taken in by a Catholic priest. Farther along, in Argentina, a customs agent in a small town told me to get the hell out of the country. I met some young revolutionaries, theater actors, in Mendoza, and whenever I remember them today, I think they certainly must have been rounded up and murdered during the Dirty War a few years later.

There were many left-leaning types on the road and even some North Americans and Europeans. I met fellow travelers while riding on the backs of flatbeds, walking the streets of the larger towns, and at archaeological sites such as Machu Picchu and beautiful natural places like General Carrera

Lake. I didn't tell anyone that I was Robert McNamara's son, and no one asked. Of course, it didn't mean that I stopped being his son. It only meant that I stopped thinking about it for a time.

There was a final ascent over a last cordillera, into Chile. I had come to my "promised land." Since the sixth grade, when my yearlong project was on Chile, I'd wanted to travel there. It was September of 1971, springtime in the Chilean valley.

9.

Santiago

In Santiago the news was all about Fidel Castro. He was visiting Chile for several weeks to take part with Salvador Allende in a celebration of Latin American socialism. Allende was Chile's new president, a freely elected socialist leader. The avenues leading up to La Moneda were packed with students, the Chilean counterparts of the Berkeley protesters, all of them chanting, *"Momio, ladrón, fascista, maricón!"*

The chant was at once radical and violent, passionate and intolerant. *Momio* referred to Chile's reactionary right-wingers. *Ladrón* means "thief," which referred to the country's wealthy landowners. *Fascista* translates easily. *Maricón* is a slur used to insult gay men. That was how the crowd chose to attack its political enemies.

I chanted along. I didn't think about the latent homophobia, which seems so vicious to me now. In the moment being in that crowd only felt like a natural progression from the protests I attended in college. I'd traveled a great distance, politically as well as geographically. Growing up with the memory of the Cuban Missile Crisis, with my dad's silver calendar a fixture in the house, I never could have guessed that eventually I was going to admire Fidel Castro more than any American political leader.

By the time I arrived in Santiago, I had decided to remain in Chile indefinitely. I really wanted a job. I thought I would try to learn more about farming, since I had been living with and working with farmers along the road south. I also wanted to live in a country with a freely elected socialist president. More than any protests in the Bay Area, these experiences differed from my family's norms and expectations. This wasn't just a different path. These were different woods.

I walked all over Santiago, peering into buildings under construction, asking for a job. Work was hard to come by. Sanctions squeezed the country. The *momios*, backed by the Chilean elite, CIA propaganda, the World Bank, and other forces of capitalism, were effective in curtailing the flow of global financing into Chile. Manufacturing was slow, agriculture was localized, and jobs were scarce. This was the era when America still believed in the bogeyman of "international Communism." We might be losing in Vietnam, but we weren't learning our lesson in Latin America either. A quote from Henry Kissinger, speaking about Chile during this period, sums up the American attitude: "I don't see why we need to stand by and watch a country go Communist due to the irresponsibility of its people." Never mind what the Chilean people actually wanted and decided through their own elections.

Compared with getting work, finding a place to live was easy. Many other gringos and Europeans, fellow travelers, had made their way to Santiago. While in line at the central post office collecting mail from the US, I met the people who would become my future housemates. They were renting a comfortable home in the hills above the city, in a district called Arrayán.

The rent was cheap. I slept on the living room floor and barely used the kitchen. Every day I'd ride the bus down to the city center and wander through the city's central market. My favorite meals always included the fresh seafood coming from Valparaiso, dishes like *locos* (abalone) and *pastel de jaiba* (crab pie). It wasn't hard to find local white wine from the Maipo Valley, perfect to pair with fresh fish. During many long days without work, without much to do, I ate and explored to stay busy. My lifestyle was part nomadic and part epicurean.

Staying in touch with my family was challenging. There were plenty of public phones, but connecting internationally was sometimes impossible. As I remember it now, there were not a lot of operators available. One evening, I stumbled into a call center and met a Chilean operator over the phone. She took an interest in the difficulty I was experiencing in connecting my call to the US, and we got to talking. This initial conversation turned into a phone romance. Over the next several months, whenever I made an international call, I hoped that by some stroke of luck she'd be my operator. Whenever I connected with her, we'd chat on the line, comparing notes on the street demonstrations that were taking place across Santiago. We talked about meeting in person, but we never did.

I desperately wanted a girlfriend. I'd been on the road for more than eight months. I had hitchhiked over four thousand miles from Bogotá to Santiago, sleeping in bus stations, on dirt floors, and under the stars in fields of squash and corn. The absence of women in my life was difficult, as it had been in boarding school. More, I wanted a relationship in order to have a direction. I felt myself languishing; I didn't feel useful.

My Spanish was improving, at least. I was going to the cafés in the mornings, reading the newspapers for practice. I was learning the history of Chile, understanding more about early Spanish colonialism, twentieth-century imperialism, and US interference. That's why I took to the streets to see Fidel Castro speak in Santiago. That's why I took up the chant. *"Momio, ladrón, fascista, maricón."* The slogan seemed to be everybody's favorite, out of the dozens that echoed across Santiago in the days leading up to Comandante Fidel's visit.

As the crowd marched down the Alameda in November of 1971 to see Castro, enveloped in the fragrance and warmth of spring, street vendors hawked *mote con huesillo.* To recharge our chanting voices, many of us bought this drink, a sweet and clear peach nectar served in a glass, with thick slices of sun-dried peaches and the *mote*—cooked husked wheat. This cooled me down, but revolutionary fervor was burning inside me. The Chilean students marching by my side had arranged themselves in brigades, carrying red banners with Fidel's profile and Cuban flags. We started to chant, *"El pueblo unido jamás será vencido!"* The people united will never be defeated.

Our destination was the Universidad Técnica del Estado.

There, Fidel was to give the first of many speeches during his stay in Chile. I stood in the crowd just a few feet below his podium. I don't remember how I managed to get so close. Fervor and excitement must have propelled me forward.

As Castro began to speak, I was spellbound. I had never heard a political leader articulate with such intensity the importance of providing universal health care and education. Castro also spoke about the evil of US domination in Latin America. With fervor, he declared, "They talk about the failure of socialism. But where is the success of capitalism in Africa, Asia, and Latin America?"

As a kid growing up in the '60s with a father in the Kennedy administration, I had been in the white-hot center of anti-Communism. The Soviets were the enemy. Fidel, we were taught, was their Latin American pawn. By the time I stood before Castro's podium, I'd completed a 180-degree turn. For three hours, with my scalp sizzling in the noonday sun, I listened in rapture to a story so different from the one I had been raised with. It wasn't about the red menace of global Communism but the plight of workers and farmers. I had been on the road for many long and dusty months, meeting subsistence farmers, hoeing their corn and beans, sleeping on their dirt floors, lighting kitchen fires before sunrise to warm milk before heading up the mountains to gather firewood, sweeping the floor with ash from the fire to make it shine. I had come to believe that farming, politics, and power are intrinsically entwined. The poorest farmer can often provide enough food for his or her family, but political instability, war, and greed are eroding that ability in modern times. The farmer is subject to the whims and winds of industrialized history, often forced to drink contaminated water, with no voice in the marketplace.

Chanting for Fidel in the streets, I was focused only on these beliefs. I didn't think about the undercurrent of hatred that informed our chanting. I was standing with my friend Gordon, a fellow traveler who had also shacked up in Arrayán. He was from Scotland. We had met at the *correo*, part of the traveler's trail, while checking for messages, and he had become my Santiago companion.

Gordon told me he was gay, but we didn't speak much about his sexuality. It didn't make a difference to me. Did it make a difference to him? He recited that chant along with the rest of us. I feel disgusted knowing that my friend heard me say that word, *maricón*. Only many years later did I become aware of the extent to which gay people were persecuted in Cuba under Castro. It hurts me to think about this, because I admired Castro so much. We were trying to form a socialist monolith in Chile, but there were mineral veins of evil in it. Gordon was dedicated to the cause, like me a supporter of Allende, and I don't know how he endured the complications of his identity.

If Robert McNamara had been the hero of my childhood, Fidel Castro held that place when I was in my early twenties. I can't reconcile the admiration I had for him with the horror I feel at his flaws. As Americans we are quick to point out when foreign leaders have a streak of evil or even shades of gray. My father, a respectable cabinet member with a clean-shaven face, was just as flawed.

I stood just feet away from Fidel Castro as he spoke to a crowd of university students in Santiago, Chile, in 1971.

One morning, I was sitting at a sidewalk café in Santiago, sipping a coffee and catching up on the news. An article in *El Mercurio*, Santiago's main newspaper, caught my eye. The United Nations was holding its Third Session on Trade and Development in Santiago. Robert S. McNamara, President of the World Bank, would be giving the keynote address.

I paused, put the paper down, and held my coffee without taking a drink. I had not seen or spoken to my father in almost a year. So many things had changed. The country I had left behind began to reappear in my memory. I recalled that I was an American. I hadn't even known that he was in Chile.

Before cell phones, and given that they had no fixed

address for me, there was no way for my family to know my whereabouts. Yet there Dad was. It almost seems like fiction, the way he caught up with me.

The power of the American Empire was now clearer to me than ever. I had traveled far, but my father's influence reached farther. Country by country, I was learning more about the role that the US played in the world.

The world education I had begun for myself placed Vietnam in a new light. It no longer seemed like a tragic mistake made by wise but flawed men. It now appeared to reflect an odious national mindset of imperialism.

Picking up the newspaper again, I found another article about my father, a humor piece. It featured a classic photo of him, probably testifying before Congress. The profile shot showed his wire-rimmed glasses tight across his pug nose, his hair combed straight back and parted in the middle, his shoulders hunched and his lips pursed like he was responding to a tough question. The caption to the photo stated: "MCNAMARA: Bought a section of Martha's Vineyard island for the 'dolce vita.'"

The accompanying column read:

Robert McNamara, current president of the World Bank and ex North American Secretary of Defense, together with friends, recently purchased an island off the coast of Massachusetts. His objective is to own a private beach where he can practice nudism. It is possible that in this environment new theories of sterilization will occur to him, which he can then offer as a prescription to Latin Americans. This is the true passion of McNamara.

There were grains of truth in this article. My mother and father, together with friends, did purchase a piece of land on Martha's Vineyard. It included Lucy Vincent Beach, the most secluded nude beach on the island, where island-goers can sneak through fields of huckleberry bushes to dive into the surf and paint their nude bodies with the gray clay from the cliffs.

My father had many concerns about sustainability that informed his work at the World Bank, and they were not separable from his love of the outdoors. I have one of his letters from the early 1990s in which he writes to a friend about global warming. He knew that it was going to become a global concern in the ensuing decades. My father was also a diehard zero-population-growth adherent. Understanding the impact of a single human life on greenhouse gas emissions, he believed governments should provide access to family planning and reproductive care. When my wife and I decided to have a third child, all he said to me was "I hope you know what you're doing."

When I put the newspaper down that morning at the café, I understood that I was not going to see my father in Santiago. Although we had traveled to the same city by chance, in our intentions we were too far apart to possibly meet.

A quarter century passed before I got to meet Fidel Castro. It was at the 1996 World Food Summit in Rome, a conference of the United Nations aimed at solving the problems of global food insecurity.

Castro's arrival in Rome was triumphant. For several days, he was the star of the summit. He branded the developed nations of the First World "hypocritical." I could relate; I'd often felt that my father, formerly president of the World Bank, had been hypocritical.

I was serving as a US delegate to the summit, and I was obligated to toe the line of diplomatic relations. Because the US had an embargo against Cuba, there was to be no communication between the delegates of the two nations. I spoke with our team leader, Assistant Secretary of State Tim Wirth, about the possibility of meeting Fidel. He said that if the occasion presented itself, he was okay with my jumping on it.

Although Castro didn't know me, he and my father were in some way intimates, having narrowly avoided a global catastrophe, on opposite sides. Both were considered criminals by their harshest critics. My father had sought to pacify a Communist country and in the process had contributed to millions of deaths while tearing a hole in his own homeland. Fidel would have sacrificed his nation, his people, and his revolution in order to oppose the United States and capitalism.

On day two of the plenary session, Fidel entered the conference building in his usual flurry of charismatic personality. He took his seat in the middle of the oval hall. A guard was posted at either end of his aisle. I hastily scribbled a note of introduction in Spanish on my yellow legal pad with the intent of showing it to the guard. From my seat, I walked down to the plenary floor. Across the hall from me was the entire US delegation, seeming to look me straight in the eye. I took a deep breath and handed my introduction to the guard. To my utter surprise, he waved me past. At that point I was breathless. My heart was pounding so much that I'm sure it could have been heard as far away as Cuba. I crouched down to the floor, avoiding any possibility of being seen, and I proceeded to crawl on all fours between the rows of auditorium seats all the way from the beginning of the aisle to its center, where Fidel Castro was. As I approached his feet, I began to rise. It was like a rebirth.

At his side was his ever-present translator, a very attractive younger woman, who stood up alongside the two of us. In Spanish, I addressed Fidel directly, introducing myself as an organic walnut and olive grower from California and a dele-gate to the World Food Summit. His eyebrows arched upward as I spoke. I sensed his interest when I mentioned farming. He seemed to believe me when I spoke of our mutual interest in and commitment to reversing global food insecurity.

When I said that I was the son of Robert McNamara, a broad smile formed in the forest of his beard. He and my father had met in Cuba in 1992, when they joined together with other Soviet and Cuban officials to discuss the historic showdown.

"I have great admiration for your father," he said.

I didn't have time for a proper reply. The plenary session was about to begin. I hastily asked if he would sign my copy of the summit program. We shook hands, and I returned to my seat, this time walking fully upright.

Things were different now that they were old men. Of course they could admire each other. They were both looking back on long careers. Of course Castro admired him. They shared a son.

I wonder if I've been too hard on my father.

Maybe I shouldn't think that. I cannot be too hard on him.

Perhaps it would have been good for us to come together

in Chile in 1972. On the other hand, he might have been too busy. What would he have thought about my transformation? Where in the city would it have been possible for an American dignitary and his left-wing, itinerant son to sit down and make conversation?

Today I know that this period was the most enlightening, engaging, and fulfilling part of my parents' lives. After 1968, Mom and Dad traveled to almost every country in the world. They met with heads of state, and they brought with them all their American hopes for prosperity, health, and human rights.

Looking back at the timing of Dad's visit to Chile, I understand that the United Nations conference, focused on free trade and spearheaded by the president of the World Bank, was a counterforce against the Castro-Allende celebration of socialism. The United States played the role of a paternalistic outsider, pushing and dragging and cajoling other countries to develop in ways amenable to American interests and ideology. As the conference was getting underway, CIA operatives were already engaged in toppling the Allende government. Meanwhile, the Vietnam War dragged on.

10.

Island, Fall

I didn't know it back then, but during my time in Chile, I was looking for family.

It was not that I wanted to disown my true family. As time in Santiago wore on, I missed my mother dearly, and I missed the good times with my father. But I felt the call to a different way of life. They were still in Washington, still managing a world from way above the soil. I was in love with farming, and I wanted to live a life close to the soil.

One day, with these feelings strong in my heart, I found myself on a bus heading to Tierra del Fuego. On the bus I met a young Argentinian couple, Carmen and Luis. They were very loving and natural people, hippies who went barefoot and dressed in lots of color. Politically, they supported Allende. They became my traveling friends.

The three of us hiked in the cordillera above Ushuaia, the southernmost city in the world. We camped in lenga forests, roasted meat over smoldering fires, boiled stews of mussels that we gathered in an estuary, and baked bread in a primitive earth oven. Those were dreamy times, and Carmen and Luis shared everything with me. At night, camping out under the stars, we slept alongside each other in a row of three.

Carmen and Luis might have been only a footnote in this story, but when I said goodbye to them, heading back to Santiago, I felt like I was saying goodbye to a piece of myself. I was in love with Carmen.

There was an obvious attraction, and we both knew it, but nobody said anything out loud. I respected and admired Luis. It had never been in my upbringing or in my character to pursue a married woman. Still, my feelings for Carmen moved at a high velocity, the same speed with which I had fled my old preoccupations in the States.

When I returned to Santiago, Carmen and I started to exchange letters. She was a watercolor painter, and she sent me paintings with each of her messages. In return, I sent her sketches. Through this correspondence, we gradually started to acknowledge being in love. It developed over distance, not unlike my crush on the phone operator. We didn't talk about her husband in our letters. We talked about what we wanted.

We both wanted to start a farm in Chile. Beyond that, we wanted family and children. Before long, we were making elaborate plans in writing. I let our long-distance relationship go on and nurtured it, even though she was married. I suppose there was an element of love for the unattainable in the way I felt about her. Carmen began to represent in my mind a new direction, toward my most deeply held desires—to be loved and understood and free from my American adolescence.

At this time, I was also planning a journey to Easter Island. There were many reasons to go. In Santiago I had become friends with a woman from the island, Maria. Her tales of the folklore of Rapa Nui intoxicated me. Maria told me that her family would be happy to host me.

Looking back, I connect the desire to travel farther with my inner search—for that yolk, which kept oozing between my fingers when I tried to grasp it. Stay in motion, move forward, away from the center of your life. This was my way. Dad showing up in Santiago must have contributed to pushing me out to sea.

I took a plane there. I had only my backpack and a Nikon camera around my neck. Maria had called ahead to tell her family on the island that a gringo was coming to visit. From the window I saw a group of people in hats woven from palm, standing just off the runway, which was an open field. They seemed to know me already, because as soon as I stepped off the plane the family came forward to greet me. Maria's aunt Vera wrapped her arms around me and draped me in necklaces of shiny marine mollusks. Within minutes, I could barely move my neck. Twenty bands of ocean shells strung together with fishing line rested on my chest.

In her native tongue, Vera greeted me: "*Lornan, pehe coi...riva riva?*"

Pascuense was the language of Easter Island, and I didn't know a word of it. There was very little English spoken there. Over the course of the next year and a half, I would learn enough Pascuense to make people laugh at my mistakes.

Vera's family lived in a large house with cinder-block walls, a good roof, and big windows that let in the island's oceanic light. Their home stood out somewhat from the majority of the smaller, wood-built houses, but it was not completely un-usual. There had been an influx of capital during the 1960s, when American GIs disembarked on Rapa Nui to monitor an atmospheric testing station. They had left behind money, various accoutrements, more than a few children, and an economic connection to North American capitalism. Consequently, it was not unusual to see a gringo on the island. Travelers were common. During my stay there, my Scottish friend Gordon visited me.

Vera lived with many adult children. Her son Isidoro was a free spirit and a free diver; he provided a lot of resources for the family by going deep into the ocean, with no scuba or snorkel gear, to catch lobsters and other shellfish. Her other son, Fernando, was close to me in age, and we developed a brotherly relationship. There was also an adult daughter in the house, Anna, who had a disability. I don't know how she would have been diagnosed in North America, but she couldn't communicate. Mama Vera's temperament was very optimistic, very joyful, despite the many responsibilities of her life and her children. She reminded me of my own mother, and her family turned into my family—a connection I desperately needed. As much as I had wanted to escape the world of my father and the controversy of Vietnam, I yearned, after so much time on the road, for the embrace of a mother.

Vera gave me a new name, Tuu Koiho, after a figure from the island's mythology. According to the local legends, Tuu Koiho was a trickster spirit who made the mo'ai statues walk from rock quarries in the mountains to their ceremonial platforms on the coast. To the best of my understanding, the nickname was an honor; at meals I often received the most desirable cuts of meat, such as the head and entrails of tuna seared over an open fire.

It's also possible that the name Tuu Koiho was given to me because I actually did have something to do with moving the mo'ai statues. For almost a year, I worked under William Mulloy, the American anthropologist and archaeologist who dedicated his life to restoring the mo'ai of Easter Island. Mulloy ran a small team of about a dozen islanders, plus me and a few other travelers. Dressed only in shorts and boots, we worked with pickaxes, shovels, and pry bars to set the altar stones of the Tahai site in place.

I was on Rapa Nui for over a year and a half, and I celebrated two birthdays with Vera's family. I had little correspondence with my friends in the States, and for a while I didn't need it. My ties to the US were threadbare. This new place seemed like a paradise to me. On my twenty-second birthday, I woke up feeling like a different man: part Chilean, part islander, someone who was not wholly of any country.

I remember preparing a great feast that day. We went to a beach called Ana Kana, one of the few sandy beaches on the rocky island, and we prepared *uma pae*, a ceremonial delicacy. The name literally means "food under earth," or "earth oven." It was a dish reserved for special events, such as a wedding or a burial. We dug a pit two meters wide and lined it with volcanic rocks. Fernando and I got a fire going in the hole. My friend Mike helped us. Together we fed the fire with new logs, adding to it every hour. We drank white wine out of five-gallon glass jugs wrapped in woven wicker, which arrived sporadically to the island by boat.

After the logs had turned to ash and the lava rocks were red-hot, we constructed an extravagant stew in the earth, stacking layers of meat and sweets and herbs and seafood and green banana leaves. We capped the concoction with a simple burlap sack and finally covered the entire pit with soil. When the cooking was complete, Vera uncovered the top-soil with a shovel and pulled back the burlap sack, revealing the first layer of banana leaves. Nobody else had this special responsibility. As the stew was uncovered, I smelled the steam and the aromas of roasting meat. We heaped everything onto wooden planks and feasted. It was the most amazing fusion of flavors and smells, made better by company and ceremony. Drunk from the party and delirious with happiness, I showed my traveler friends how I'd learned to climb a coconut tree, wrapping myself around the trunk and using the sections of the bark as footholds. Clinging on with three limbs at the top, trying to shake a coconut loose, I nearly fell several times. This was only one of my thrill-seeking activities on the island, along with free-climbing on the seaside cliffs and riding horses bareback in the night. The thought that I could be in any danger was so far from my mind. The motorcycle accident in Mexico was in the distant past. Even more remote was the fear of being drafted.

Toward the middle of my stay, I moved out of Vera's house and went looking for a more permanent place, because I felt that I might be on the island indefinitely. Another family, the Haoas, allowed me to live on their land in a pasture with some dairy cows and a wooden shack that could serve as a house. Before long, I discovered that I preferred to live in a nearby cave.

Rapa Nui has an intricate cave system. Most of the caves are shaped like long corridors or tubes, formed by lava flows and large bubbles of volcanic gas. I chose the particular cave where I lived for its size—the mouth was about the height of a house door—and for its location, facing the ocean and the

Ahu Vai Uri, a platform of mo'ai statues. There was enough room in there for a bed of blankets. I moved stones and logs to serve as furniture. This was the most decorating I had done since my childhood bedroom in Washington, where I hung the US flag upside down and displayed punji stakes. I had an entirely different mindset now. Survival was always front of mind. I was living a subsistence lifestyle with no running water, no electricity, and no septic system. My concerns were for the day at hand, no more.

One challenge was gathering adequate drinking water. The shack outside my cave caught rain in a cistern roof, and I gathered the rainwater in the mornings. Heavy rain also brought flooding. When my friend Gordon stayed with me, we weathered many tropical storms together, sometimes evacuating the cave and sleeping in the shack. When we wanted adventure, we woke early in the morning and rode horses around the island, camping out together for days. At one point I traded a pair of Levi's jeans, which my mother had shipped to me, in order to purchase my own horse. That this was considered a fair trade shows the extent to which American products had infiltrated Rapa Nui. In bartering, American cigarettes also went a long way. Perhaps that's how I managed to procure a speargun to hunt for lobster and fish in the surf. The danger was getting out of the water without getting rolled onto the point of the spear by a big wave.

Remembering this time, I have tried to imagine my father's life in the United States while I was on the island. The Pentagon Papers controversy was probably the biggest development in his story. While I was traveling, I had no idea about this. I knew that Dad had come to Chile, but I had no sense of how he was dealing with the ongoing controversies surrounding the Vietnam War. Later in life, I never had a proper conversation with Dad about the Pentagon Papers. In his memoir, *In Retrospect*, he describes in somewhat generic terms the effect the report had on him—coming under scrutiny and enduring criticism. From what I know about his career at the World Bank, he was putting all of his time and energy into global economic development—and, of course, tipping the scales in favor of global capitalism.

Years later, I would desperately yearn to learn directly from my father about this period of his career. But on Easter Island I was totally uninformed, and happy to be so. I had no idea of the extent to which my father had withheld his doubts about the war from me and from the country—the extent to which he had lied, all along, about the idea that we could win.

The influence of global economics was felt on Rapa Nui. In response to beef shortages in Santiago, islanders slaughtered their own horses and sent the meat over the sea. I never did the actual deed. I would watch someone else, maybe Isidoro, point a pistol between the beautiful eyes of a horse and pull the trigger, watch it tumble to the ground and writhe. Once the animal was down, someone slit its throat. The group of us—I assisted in this part—caught the warm blood in a big black tub, to be used later to make blood sausages. A team of men sawed the carcass, first removing the legs, then the hide. I remember how a gentle breeze would come up from the coast just a hundred feet away from the open-air *palapa* where the butchering happened. It made me nauseated. Remembering it now, I see how different the experience was from marveling at mule bodies on the mountain slopes of the Sierras. I was less removed.

There were so many animals on the island. Sheep roamed freely, and there were many cows. To my eyes it seemed that the islanders had everything they needed. Yet when I first arrived on Rapa Nui, the locals preferred not to drink fresh cow milk. Instead they imported powdered milk. This created a unique opportunity for me. Using loose stones from the field, I constructed a pen for the dairy cows owned by the Haoa family, which were grazing right outside my cave. These were healthy animals, always munching on guavas and taro tops. I asked my neighbors if they would allow me to begin a small dairy cooperative, and they assented.

Gordon was my first partner. He and I had to teach ourselves how to milk cows. The principal difficulty was securing the cow. I learned how to tie the cow's hind legs loosely together to stop her from stepping into the milk pail. Early on, we ruined many pails by placing them too far behind the udder. Those big, sloppy, wet cow pies would fall directly into our fresh milk.

At first we thought that the local families would participate in milking in exchange for free milk. It turned out that the islanders were happier to have us milk the cows for them and to pay for the milk to be delivered, which provided me with a small income. After milking each day, we would put most of the milk into repurposed wine jugs wrapped in woven wicker. We tied the jugs on each side of a horse's saddle, like the saddlebags on mules during my family's pack trips in the Sierras. For months I delivered the milk on horseback, liter by liter, to my rural neighbors. As I steered my horse along red, dusty paths of volcanic dirt, I'd yell out: "*Ua aapi, ua aapi*" ("Fresh milk, fresh milk"). With a funnel in hand, I would fill my neighbors' smaller bottles as they came out to meet me. Before long I became known as the milkman.

In the afternoons, we used our extra milk to make cheese. The islanders showed me how to do this. They would take the stomach of a slaughtered calf, dry it, slice it into pieces, put it into a bucket of whey, and add peppers and other ingredients to make a culture. For someone living in a cave for a year without running water or electricity, this was a great way to obtain protein. With a banana plant growing just outside the cave, I had all the food I needed.

As evening turned to dark blue, my fire lit the lava walls of my *ana*, my cave. Another day passing. I watched the sunsets from the *ana*. On one occasion, I observed the Emerald Flash. This was a legendary phenomenon, a green shimmer of light that occurs just before the last part of the sun sinks below the horizon of the ocean. I'd heard about it from other travelers. Watching the Flash gave me a profound sense of fulfillment. I was realizing with my own eyes what had been a dream. It made me feel as though anything could be accomplished.

Surely Lyndon Johnson, if he had known about my peregrinations, would have thought that living in a cave and milking cows was a strange fate for Bob McNamara's young son. But during those many months, thoughts like that didn't come to me. I didn't have news of the war or regular correspondence. The letters I got were mostly from Carmen and my mother. The island's one phone was unreliable. I didn't know that Nixon and Kissinger were escalating the war and extending US bombing into Cambodia and Laos. I was living in a tunnel underground, but I didn't think about the Viet Cong soldiers digging tunnels to ambush US troops or shelter from US mortar fire. The only real reminder I had of war was the occasional flyover spraying of pesticide by the Chilean government, which was trying to get rid of fruit flies on Easter Island. When I heard those planes from my cave, the hum of the engines, I felt briefly that turmoil had returned to my life. But when I stepped out of the cave, the planes were gone. Except for these brief interruptions, the sky above the ocean where I fished and the green fields where I rode held only endless dreams.

Ua aapi *(fresh milk)* on Easter Island

Packages sent to Easter Island from the States took three to six months to arrive. Despite the distance, the mail delivery on remote Rapa Nui worked remarkably well. I could count on getting care packages from my loving mother. As sure as the sun would rise each day, they would come. The packages she sent me contained what Mom considered the staples: letters, Hershey's chocolate bars (the kind with almonds), and packages of Stim-U-Dents for cleaning my teeth. I still carry a small package of these in my car for on-the-road dental hygiene.

In my farm office, I have one of Mom's handwritten letters from one of these packages. As hard as I've tried, it's impossible now to read her spidery handwriting. I imagine that at the time I was better able to interpret her words. Probably the most important thing was just having that small connection to home, an assurance that she was there for me. I didn't receive letters from my father, and I can't imagine what he thought of having a son who had wandered so far off the beaten path.

My emotions, whenever I thought about home, were a mess. Dreaming from within my cave, I didn't find the clarity and inner light that I had expected to discover when setting out from Palo Alto. I only discovered that the darkness and confusion in my heart had contours and a personality all their own.

On extremely rare occasions, I'd try to make a call from the only public phone on Rapa Nui back to Washington, DC. I can hear my mother's voice today as it sounded when we connected over that international line: sparkling, chipper, masking her concern for me.

"When do you think you might come home?"

"I don't know, Mom."

Perhaps these conversations influenced her to come to Easter Island. I never expected this to happen, but she made the long journey, alone. With Vera, I stood on the runway to greet my mother just as I had been greeted when I arrived. We draped dozens of *peepee* and *puri* shells around Mom's neck. Vera gave her a sun hat made from banana and palm fronds. It was the first time I'd seen my mother in a year and eight months.

We spent a week together. On horseback, then on foot, we climbed to the top of the volcano Rano Kau. On the rim of the volcano, we found petroglyphs of Tangata Manu and Make-Make, spirits of the island, which had been carved in the frozen lava. We made rubbings of these images by laying thick sheets of cotton over the petroglyphs and spreading a local paste over the cloth, capturing the figures. I hoped that Mom would share these with Dad and that she would fill him in on all the wonderful things I was doing. It wasn't so hard, with her there, to imagine him being there too. He was a good outdoorsman; he would have enjoyed the hiking and riding, making campfires and drinking wine in jugs.

As quickly as she arrived, Mom returned home. It was a remarkably long way for her to travel for such a short visit. I think that she needed to check in, to make sure I was surviving. I don't remember exactly what I felt as I said goodbye to her. Before she boarded the plane, I am certain that she must have said something in parting to remind me that she and Dad were still there.

You can come home anytime. We'll be ready.

I felt some joy because she'd traveled around the world to find me, demonstrating again how much she loved me. There was also sadness, because I knew she was suffering—from ulcers and from loneliness, with none of her children still in the house, still accompanying my father's walks through the hallways of world power. I felt that I should return home to support her and return her love, but I didn't want to go back.

I began to feel torn between love of the island and the

love I still had for my family. It deepened as I thought about Mom's reasons for visiting. Lying in the cave or the shack or in the grass under the stars at night, I asked myself, *If I stay in South America, if I start a family here, if I never go back to the United States, will that mean losing my parents?*

I recently found a journal entry from Rapa Nui, from shortly after Mom's visit.

I love my mom and pop. It's going to be really hard to relate to them when I return. In my dreams, I had a fantasy conversation with Dad on a bus ride crossing the gray lands of Tierra del Fuego. In it I told him all the truths I could think of, all the feelings that I've never spoken. And I didn't really feel better, but at least I thought more profoundly of the truth.

Rereading this, my eyes focus on the words *when I return.* I must have known that I would eventually go back to the States, even if I still had no plane ticket.

And there's the other thing: truth. Only in my dreams. It took years and years for me to understand how dysfunctional my family was with respect to speaking the truth. We didn't know how to communicate. To this day, I can't imagine what my indefinite absence was like for my parents. I've experienced times of fear and uncertainty when my own children have been away from me. Yet I can't compare that to my father's isolation and fall from grace in the 1970s. I wonder if my prolonged absence contributed to what was surely a time of great guilt for him, setting him up for depression in his later years.

Back then I felt so strongly that my father knew the truth and kept it from me. Now I'm not sure I can define *truth*.

It was more than what Dad obscured in his misleading statements, and it was more than his inadequate apologies. It was more than what any false utterance could hide. The truth I was writing about in that journal was a feeling, more than any one idea. It's what I needed from my family that I didn't get. It's like any unfulfilled promise: of a country to its citizens, of a person to their own ideals. That need for the thing that you're not quite sure is really there. That's probably why I dreamed of meeting Dad on the bus, the place where I'd met Carmen.

Thousands of miles, two continents, and much ocean separated us, but what still separated us most was that difficult word.

Nowhere is paradise, and Rapa Nui was no exception. There was political upheaval, and I became increasingly aware of it. The local people, I came to understand after living there for over a year and a half, were troubled by being treated unequally by the Chilean government. There was also inequality among the islanders themselves, which I discovered through my friendship with Francisco. He was one of a small number of Rapa Nui residents afflicted with leprosy.

Long before I arrived, people like Francisco, his family and community, had been shuttled off to an isolated colony miles from the main town. Taboos and fears of leprosy had waned somewhat with the introduction of modern medicine. However, when I was on the island, there was still a separation. Most of the members of the colony, feeling shunned by the rest of the islanders, chose to remain in their wooded enclave.

Francisco was one of the island's best wood carvers. For

135

his sculptures he carved from traditional Toromiro wood, a type of mimosa bush. He had only one hand and one leg, on opposite sides, and it was remarkable to witness him at work. He braced the block of Toromiro on the right side of his groin as he carved downward with his left arm. For each statue, he would use a rasp made of shaped coral or a chunk of a ray's tail to smooth out the rough areas of a chosen piece of wood. From there he carved with blades of polished stone and obsidian knives. For delicate curves and accents, he used a rat's tooth or small shark teeth. Final polishing was done with dried ray's skin and finished with wet sand.

Francisco gave me a sculpture of a swordfish, which I still have. When I first held it in my hands, I was amazed at his craftsmanship. More than that, I felt a powerful admiration for him and gratitude for being welcomed into his life. I felt such hope whenever I spent time with Francisco. Yet something was still missing. Despite all the new experiences I had accumulated, I still couldn't find my inner yolk, that personal resource and foundation I imagined for myself. There was a long way left for me to go, and it wasn't a distance that could be measured only in miles.

A final run-in with the local carabineros, the national police force of Chile, which had jurisdiction over the entire national territory, was the last straw for me. As far as I could tell, the islanders of Rapa Nui resented the carabineros, who were the boots on the ground for a government that treated them unequally. One of the biggest disagreements concerned sheep. There were thousands of sheep roaming semi-freely over the grasslands of Rapa Nui. Vera told me that the first flock of sheep to arrive on the island was a gift to the islanders from the bishop of Tahiti. Starting in the 1950s, foreign companies and the Chilean government used the island to cultivate ever-growing numbers of sheep and export the wool. But once the islanders gained full Chilean citizenship, it was their belief that the sheep belonged to them, not the Chilean government.

I remember riding bareback under the night sky with a small band of wranglers looking for sheep. Vera's son Fernando probably introduced me to this activity. Galloping past the dark silhouettes of mo'ai silently standing watch over the land, we held lassos, ready to rope a furry animal and sling it over our horses. The act had a name: *toki toki*, meaning "stealing." I think my wrangler friends thought it was just harvesting what was rightfully theirs.

I didn't think about getting caught, only about the speed of the horses and the excitement of successfully lassoing a sheep. This was the fastest I moved on the island; it fed my love of speeding through life. After one of our night rides, the carabineros suspected that I was involved with *toki toki*. I was hauled into the police encampment, and it was made clear to me that my visa to remain on Rapa Nui would be revoked. After they let me go, I started planning my departure.

Before I left Easter Island, I saw Carmen again. She came to visit me after many letters, and she came alone. We had fallen in love, and our love deepened on the island.

We rode horses together. By now I knew the best places to ride and camp. While we explored together, we made a plan to live in Chile. Allende's country was the perfect place for us to start a small family farm. We talked about the future, slept in the cave, and enjoyed the beauty of the island by day. I showed Carmen the mo'ai statues. We summited the volcano

Rano Kau together, which I had also done with Mom, and we looked down on the whole landscape together and had no fear of the future.

Luis was not with her. I assumed at the time that their relationship was over. Remembering this now, I realize that I really did want to create a life with Carmen. It wasn't just a vague dream in letters. It wasn't a fling, nor was it merely a way for her to leave her marriage. Ours was a compelling new relationship, and we felt that we could do the things we talked about. Together, we could support the *lucha*—the fight for land rights—that Salvador Allende had set in motion. Our love was a way forward, I thought, and it offered me clarity of purpose. If I couldn't find my yolk, perhaps I could create a new identity by binding myself to another person, in another place. Carmen and I made these plans over the campfires where we roasted fish and lobster fresh from the sea, and we were happy.

Things might have continued along these lines, but I needed to go home first. My mother's visit, not long before Carmen's arrival, had made me aware of a certain invisible umbilical cord. I was filled with the desire to see my mother, the rest of my family, and my friends. In my mind, I thought of this as a goodbye visit. I would go to America, inform everyone that I was now Chileno, and then return to my adopted country.

Carmen was happy to stay on Easter Island and wait for me. I planned to go back to Santiago, fly to Washington, and then fly back to Chile within a few months. It seemed like a very firm plan at the time. But now, looking back, I have doubts. If I was so in love with Carmen and so determined to live in Chile, why did I leave? Maybe I thought I could freeze our relationship in time. Maybe I wanted to stop that story from unfolding, which was what I had wanted when I left America.

Within days of saying goodbye to Carmen, boarding the plane, and returning to Santiago, I received word from Rapa Nui that she had fallen from her horse while descending from the volcano. She suffered a compound leg fracture, and there was no way that the bone could be set on Easter Island. She was bound up on a stretcher and loaded onto the next flight to the mainland.

I met her at the airport. She limped off the plane, supported by crutches. Her leg was horribly swollen, and her courageous and loving smile overwhelmed me. My mind started to race. I'd been in many adverse situations on the road, but this was the most extreme. We needed to find a doctor.

It was June 29, 1973. Santiago was in complete lockdown because of *El Tanquetazo*, a coup attempt against Allende. By taxi, Carmen and I rode from one hospital to the next. Everyone was either on strike or sheltering in place. Hobbling from clinic to clinic, Carmen somehow managed to handle her pain. Our plans were crumbling; Salvador Allende was under attack; my adopted country was hemorrhaging; and the woman I loved was broken. As I remember it, there was machine-gun and tank fire all around the city.

We finally found a doctor who agreed to operate and set the broken leg. Meanwhile I called around the city to find a place for us to stay. Some friends from my first stint in Santiago eventually connected me with a Chilean writer who lived in an A-frame house in the neighborhood of Arrayán, and he generously took us in.

That night Carmen and I lay side by side on the lower

floor of the house in Arrayán. I remember her moaning in pain through the night. The next day, Luis arrived. I had called him, because I was still planning to go home. He slept in the loft of the A-frame, with Carmen and me sleeping together below, and her pain only increased. The operation didn't seem to have helped. Months later, after intense swelling of her leg, Carmen would discover that the doctor who had set her leg was a hand surgeon. Her leg would have to be rebroken and set anew.

I loved Carmen, yet I had left her alone on the island, where she was injured. I wanted to be with her, yet I was planning to leave her again. Luis, returning to her, showed a different kind of love. Deep down, I still had no idea where I was supposed to be, but he clearly knew that he needed to be with her. I can't imagine what it was like for the two of them after I left. To this day I don't know what she told Luis about visiting me on Rapa Nui. God knows what he thought about me. God knows what became of them.

The next morning, as I got on the plane, leaving her in his arms, part of me understood that I wasn't coming back. I remember feelings of overwhelming sadness, fear, and guilt: guilt because of my effect on Carmen, fear for her physical and emotional survival, and sadness because our dream was falling apart.

It was not long after this that Salvador Allende was assassinated, on September 11, 1973. The right-wing leader who replaced him, Augusto Pinochet, was supported by Nixon. The World Bank, headed by my father, resumed lending in Chile. When he came under criticism years later for allowing the Bank to favor the brutal Pinochet regime, Dad told a *New York Times* reporter, "We have not in this institution allowed our lending policy to be determined by civil rights considerations, whether they be civil rights considerations in leftist or rightist governments."

At the time, I knew the US was complicit in the September coup. I didn't know the extent of my father's complicity. Looking at his quote now, I find it to be an abhorrent evasion. How could he claim to be an international civil servant focused on addressing global food insecurity, and an alumnus of the Great Society administration—and at the same time disregard civil rights?

To me, this is an example of a lie. It was a deliberate evasion, a strategic silence. Just as he had at the Pentagon, Dad sang the official line of that cruel Chilean policy.

These are the notes in my journal from the day after Allende was assassinated.

September 12, 1973

My soul is weeping, and my heart is anguished. My companero is dead. So many people's companero is dead. So many desires have been kindled, so many fights have begun.

New York Times, Washington Star, how can you say he should have turned back, that he didn't have the popular support? You wait and see. Chile is bound for hardship under a fascist military junta.

My grief is somewhat shadowed by violence and the desire to continue "la lucha." My passion for Chile and Allende and my companeros consumes me....Companero Allende, you will never be forgotten. Your words give me strength. Companero, I will never give up la lucha, si la lucha es con fusil.

Chile, your struggle abounds in me, I must be with you....

We have seen and lived a moment with Allende, and it will live forever....

I was hearing the bell. I was serious about going back there and taking up arms.

Despite what I wrote in my journal, I did not return. Certainly I did not take up *fusil*. For the next year, I sent money to friends in Chile who opposed Pinochet, but the money I sent didn't change the course of history.

Did my mother try to talk me out of doing that? Did I even mention the coup to my parents? I can't remember. There's no way I spoke about it with my dad. I mostly remember the sadness of a dream that ended too soon.

I often fantasized about returning to fight against the Pinochet military. I didn't make that choice, and I realize that I wasn't a true revolutionary. Yet it feels as though a few different events and a few different chance meetings might have bent me toward revolution. Had I gone back to Chile, I wonder what would have happened.

Whatever the case may be, the things I experienced in Latin America filled my soul for decades. I came away from that time a more complete person. The downside is that it left me very disconnected from the politics of my home country. Even the divisive atmosphere of the Vietnam era had not made me realize what I learned there: I was born the citizen of an empire. Ours wasn't a free country for everybody, and America had actively done things to make the rest of the world less free. After witnessing the bright star of a socialist president falling from the sky, I was determined not to participate.

11.

Return

I returned to the States in the summer of 1973. I don't remember one moment about the long flight to Miami. I must have slept the whole way. The first thing I do remember is getting off the plane. I found my way to Miami Seaport customs, where I retrieved Boojum, my motorcycle. I had shipped it back to the US many months before. It was in storage, awaiting my arrival, and it was not in good shape. The tires were worn and flat and needed replacing. Also, the wheels were completely out of alignment. At higher speeds, the bike vibrated, making it difficult to steer.

All I wanted was to be home. With Boojum shaking beneath me, I started on the road back to Washington.

Somewhere around Kingsland, Georgia, home of the annual Catfish Festival, I pulled into a filling station. It was around 9 p.m., still sweltering—July in the South. Exhausted and beaten up by the vibration of the bike, I asked the station attendant if I could sleep on the grass behind the building.

"No fucking way you're sleeping here, Goldilocks."

That was in reference to my long hair and beard.

"Thanks anyway," I said, and hopped back on my bike.

Normally I would have been able to just shrug off his comment. But the guy's words really pissed me off. I rode on in a quiet rage that was matched by the shaking of the motorcycle. I hadn't been back in the US for more than a day, and this was the welcome I got. One of the very first people I ran into happened to be a hippie hater. I started to feel that I shouldn't have come back stateside. Remembering it now, I think of veterans who returned from Vietnam and faced resentment and hatred from antiwar protesters.

When I did finally get home to Washington, things got a little better—for a time. I was greeted with such love and joy by my family and friends. For the first few days, I hardly went anywhere or did anything; life was like one big exhale. Later, going about town, eating at American restaurants, and drinking American beer again, I felt relieved and accomplished, as if I had returned from an arduous journey as a changed man.

Despite the relief I felt from being home, I was also uncomfortable. Everything seemed different, exotic. Walking into a large grocery store was completely overwhelming. The abundance and variety of foods stunned me—and this was after I'd spent weeks and weeks hanging out at Santiago markets. There were just so many different packages to choose from, so many different processed foods. I found myself staring at rows of shelves, contemplating all the manufacturing, packaging, and transportation involved in the various supply chains.

People bought and sold things in Chile and on Easter Island, just as people buy and sell things all over the world, but our hulking American warehouses of product, product,

product were surreal. Clothing retailers and furniture outlets were particularly difficult to walk around in. In the homes of my friends, and even in my own house, I marveled at how the refrigerators were so big that you could sleep in one. After growing up in the 1950s and '60s, I became aware for the first time of midcentury American material abundance—its privileges and horrors.

It didn't take me long at home to realize that I was at a crossroads again. It had been the war in Vietnam that most motivated me to leave the US, and the war was still going on. Having just come back, I found myself in a place that was neither here nor there. Returning to my childhood bedroom with all my Vietnam "souvenirs," I felt that nothing had been resolved.

But I had discovered farming; that was different. I truly loved growing things, harvesting them, and learning about plants. I knew now that I wanted to be a farmer. I had learned this from the road. That development was a late entry in the ongoing drama with my father, which had started way back in that phone booth at St. Paul's. All the love and travel and the myths of Rapa Nui hadn't changed the fact that I still lived much of my life in that small space.

In March of 1972, while I was still in Chile, three white males were arrested in a garage in Berkeley, California, after police responded to a report of gas fumes. Upon arrival, they discovered a massive homemade-bomb factory. The arsenal consisted of hundreds of pounds of explosives: gunpowder, fuses, blasting caps, and a three-gallon chemical bomb. There were also small arms, ammunition, and rifles (including an AK-47). Police discovered a quantity of fraudulent identification and a corpus of revolutionary literature, guerrilla warfare manuals, and technical materials on the manufacture and use of explosives. There were also some hand-drawn maps and plans of my family's house in Snowmass, Colorado—the same house that was under construction when I confronted the peaceful protesters at our front door in Aspen five years earlier.

The plan behind this operation, it turned out, was to kidnap Robert McNamara from his mountain home, assassinate him, and then blow the house to bits. The most illuminating find in the pile of evidence collected by police was a detailed analysis of my father, mother, and me. It was a kind of makeshift dossier, and it emphasized our athletic and physical capabilities.

Robert (called Bob by locals; or Mr. Mac) about 6' tall—appears quite strong & healthy (possibly due to his new position)—is lanky and generally near-sighted (thus the wire specs). A good skier. Hikes with his wife and/or son Craig. Robert and wife also go alone occasionally on hikes around the area (also in other wilderness areas of the U.S.). Christmas is a good time to meet them, or in summer for a wilderness hike.

Son: Craig—Long black hair & beard—wears wire specs, resembles father. Excellent skier, mountaineer. Quite strong & alert. About 5'11." Smokes dope, friendly, very open.

P.S. Go to nearest Shell Service Station and get free road map of area.

The set of documents also included a rundown of the frequency of police patrols around the Snowmass house, the depth of surveillance, and the "capability of local individuals and groups to provide assistance," with attention to their mountain-climbing abilities.

The documents read like something concocted under the influence. But this was no joke. These revolutionaries were serious—or at least seriously thinking—about catching my parents unawares. When I first read the dossier, besides reacting to the overwhelming strangeness of it, I felt troubled at being compared side by side with Dad. They even noted how I looked like him. There was irony in this for me, because I spent the early 1970s trying to distance myself from my father. Although I had shifted in my politics and had lived in a way so far from his environment in Washington, I retained his face and his name. The would-be bombers thought I was a nice guy, but they didn't know how bitterly opposed to the Vietnam War I was.

Who compiled these notes? The Berkeley Police Department report, dated June 22, 1972, and sent to my father, states that one of the three men arrested in the garage, William Brandt, "is acquainted with an unknown subject who is acquainted with your son and who provided Brandt with the material on your home and family." Someone I knew was channeling information to the revolutionary army with the intent of murdering my father. I'll never know who it was.

I later learned that Willie Brandt was the boyfriend of Wendy Yoshimura, who was renting out the garage to the would-be bombers. Willie introduced her to the Symbionese Liberation Army (SLA). I have to assume that he was acquainted with someone from Bay Area circles who knew me.

Wendy is a Japanese-American artist who was born in an internment camp during World War II. She grew up mostly in California. She became involved in revolutionary activities in the early 1970s. In 1975 she was arrested in San Francisco along with Patty Hearst, the granddaughter of the newspaper mogul William Randolph Hearst. Both of them were associated with the SLA. Wendy was eventually put on trial.

During the trial, my father contacted me to see if I would testify before a judge that the maps of the Snowmass house and the descriptions of him, Mom, and me were indeed correct. In effect, he was asking me to testify against Wendy Yoshimura. I wouldn't have had to do much besides confirm simple facts, but I felt conflicted about Dad's request.

Considering whether to testify, I saw myself in the meadow in Aspen, surrounded by the war protesters. I remembered how I could see myself in them; they had been an incredibly calm, peaceful, and ultimately inspiring group. I remembered my first stint in college, when I went to sit-ins, performed guerrilla theater in lecture halls, and occupied administration buildings. I recalled the hatred that had been directed at me while I read the names of soldiers killed in Vietnam in the San Francisco Airport. I remembered the call to my father from the wooden phone booth at boarding school, when he didn't provide me with the thing I had asked for.

I could not bring myself to testify. In my place, my aunt Katie (my mother's only sibling) went to court to swear that the descriptions were correct. I assume that my decision not to testify must have felt like a significant betrayal—like I wasn't loyal. If this is true, my dad gave no indication that he felt differently about me. His loyalty to me remained intact. I want to think that he understood the justice of my choice; I was repeating what he had done to me when he left me alone to confront the protesters. That abandonment was now matched.

Did I abandon him? Was I derelict in my duty to our family? I remembered the assassination attempts he survived in the 1960s; I felt now, as I did then, that I would have fought anyone who tried to hurt him. Yet I chose not to stand by him in the trial.

Those contradictions were just normal, like the binding ties in our family. That, and our love of the outdoors. We went back to our old ways when I got back from Chile. The Snowmass house wasn't blown up, and Dad and I continued to enjoy skiing together. In the outdoors it was easier to forget our differences.

I remember being on a road trip with my parents in Jackson Hole, Wyoming. It was just the three of us, with my grown-up sisters living their own lives in different places. We were on the way to Colorado. It was a midsummer drive, with heavy rain and gusts of wind shaking the car. My father was at the wheel. Around this time, Mom had just gone through the third or fourth operation to address her ulcers. As we drove, the ulcers started to affect her. Perhaps she was feeling acute stress from driving in that weather. Maybe it was the buildup of time and the operations.

She was in so much pain. Rarely in my life had I ever seen her cry. She started to weep and to moan softly, and I felt smaller than a child. Not much time had passed since I had left Carmen behind in a state like that. To see a parent in such deep pain, having suffered the same symptoms, made me so afraid for all of us.

We pulled off the road to comfort her. Dad became quiet, which was his way during times like this. He clutched his hands together, a protective gesture and a sign of being at a loss. From the back seat, I put my hand on Mom's shoulder. I don't remember what we said to comfort her.

Once we were back on the road, I thought about all the similar incidents that must have occurred while I was gone. While I was hunting lobster, riding my horse, and delivering milk, Mom must have felt pain like this. Drinking milk to try to relieve it.

This was the first time I was really glad to have returned home.

12.

Soil

I first laid eyes on the Three Sisters in the Sierra Madre, north of Mexico City. As my BMW motorcycle bumped along dusty paths leading through fields in the lowlands of Costa Rica, I saw the Sisters again. I got more acquainted as I hitchhiked across the altiplano of the Andes.

The Three Sisters are the three principal crops of the Americas: winter squash, maize, and climbing beans. They have been grown by indigenous peoples for thousands of years. They grow together in a truly symbiotic process. The big corn seeds take root at the center of a dirt mound, forming a sturdy base. This supports the growth of the climbing beans and the flowering squash. As the beans grow, they produce nitrogen that fertilizes the maize and squash. As the squash spreads along the ground, it forms a living mulch, creating a microclimate that retains moisture in the soil. The leaves of the squash also block out sunlight, preventing weeds from taking over. The prickly, hairy texture of the leaves deters pests.

During my travels in South America, I lived with many families who cultivated the Three Sisters. When I stayed in the homes of Quechua farmers, they were a staple of every meal. Meeting farmers from Chile, I learned to refer to beans using the word *poroto*. *Poroto* is a word unique to Chile, southern Peru, and Argentina. It comes from the Quechua word for bean: *purutu*. I was continually amazed at the importance of those three crops, and the way they could sustain so many people.

I know that the farmers who took me in experienced the Sisters in a way that was utterly different from the view of a North American college dropout, who saw the life of a subsistence farmer growing these three crops in a poetic cooperative process as an uplifting departure from capitalism. To me, the Three Sisters were an incredible, romantic metaphor for sustainability and a natural way of life. Yet I know that for those families, life was neither natural nor unnatural; it was just life, the often-harsh reality of living hand to mouth. The year was spent planning for the year ahead, and the Three Sisters were always part of the plan.

In the Andes, several families allowed me to stay in their homes. The bedrooms slept four or five people, maybe six, with family members of varying ages. The houses were always neat and tidy and largely empty, with no more furniture than a closet hewed from rough pine. Often the family outhouse was placed over a running stream or rivulet of flowing water, to carry excrement downstream.

Despite my wide-eyed wonder at discovering subsistence farming, I was aware of how political forces created certain outcomes for indigenous farmers. Most farmers whom I met didn't produce much of a surplus to take to market.

In order to purchase goods like sugar, building materials, tools, and bikes, they had to trade goods made from sheep wool or other animal products. If they had cheese and other dairy products from a cow or goat, that could also be used to barter.

After I returned to the United States, I wanted to incorporate the lessons of the Three Sisters into a career in agriculture. I couldn't help being North American, and the son of a onetime industrialist, but I thought that my experiences could guide me. By becoming a small farmer, I would try to live out in my daily life the fundamental economic and political lessons I had gained from my travels.

Dad, on the other hand, was driving relentlessly forward in his career at the World Bank. If he had bothered to ask me, he might have gained perspective on the lives of the subsistence farmers he claimed to advocate for—the people I had met and lived with.

I understood the depth of his failures as the architect of Vietnam. I knew that, despite his outward silence and confidence, he was burdened by his mistakes and his regrets. I wanted a more sustainable career for myself.

In an effort to better understand localized farming practices, I traveled to Mexico for most of 1973 and 1974. It was my second journey out of the US, and it took place just a few months after I had returned from Chile. Twenty-four now, I retained my farming dreams, but I remained deeply uncomfortable in the United States. Stanford had lost its appeal, and I was not ready to give college another try. Up until September of 1973, it had truly been my goal to return to Chile and reunite with Carmen. The Pinochet takeover ultimately destroyed that dream. I was neither ready to be back in the States nor able to return to my adopted home country. As I flew south, bound for Mexico City, I hoped to discover a new experience that would bring me closer to farming.

In Mexico City I stayed in the Friends House, a Quaker hostel, where I met Walter Illsley. Walter had left the United States because of his Communist sympathies; he had served as an engineer in Mao's China in the 1940s. Now he lived with his wife and their six children in Uruapan, Michoacán. On Walter's advice, I traveled to Michoacán and ended up in a pueblo called Tomendán. There, I looked for the farming experience I needed.

Tomendán is nestled up against hills of volcanic soil, its fields golden with sugar cane. In the lands around the town, the pine and oak and dry shrubs stretch as far as the eye can see. When I first saw the pueblo, I thought it looked like a Garden of Eden, with edible plants and fruit-bearing trees dotting the countryside. Soon after I arrived there, a friend of Walter's named Raoul welcomed me into a chocolate-brown adobe house.

Raoul and his brother Emmanuel were sugar-cane farmers. One morning I ventured out from Raoul's house and came upon their group of campesinos, resting after a morning of difficult work. I must have looked strange to them. Was I the first gringo in years to walk into their town? My huaraches were old and covered in mud like theirs. But my long hair and beard, together with my backpack, certainly gave me away.

I explained to Raoul that I wanted to work alongside the group, to cultivate and harvest the cane. I told them that I wanted to be a farmer, and that I'd work for free. My Spanish wasn't perfect, but I must have tried to tell the whole story:

how I'd recently returned to the US from Chile but couldn't stay in El Norte, how I wanted an understanding of cooperative farming, and how I'd traveled south again, to this remote village in Michoacán, to find it.

I remember that the two brothers stepped aside and discussed my offer. They asked their fellow campesinos to weigh in. A few nodded their heads. Someone said that they could use the help because these were hard times. Then, in a very respectful manner, Emmanuel told me that they needed to think about my offer. He suggested that I, too, should reconsider. They told me to come back in a few days. I didn't know if they were hesitant about bringing me on or if they just couldn't believe someone wanted to work for free. Maybe they wanted to see if I would keep my word. When I returned, what could they say?

Raoul and Emmanuel first put me to work in the *piloncillo* factory. *Piloncillo* means "little loaf." It refers to a variety of boiled, hardened, and refined sugar cane with a smoky, earthy taste. *Piloncillo* has more flavor than brown sugar, and it's also healthier, with several immunological benefits. In Mexico, *piloncillos* have been made for more than five hundred years. By the time I arrived, the ejido—the state-owned, communal farm—had been operating for two years. Before that, it had been a hacienda.

Everyone specialized in a different part of the process behind *piloncillo* production. I helped operate a thirty-foot waterwheel, used to crush huge mountains of freshly harvested sugar cane into juice. Others brought fuel for the wood fires that heated the long vats from below. A few workers poured the heated juice into the molds, and the rest bagged the completed product.

The sugar-cane mill had many uses. At sunrise, the women of Tomendán took buckets of corn soaked in limewater up to the mill to be ground into *masa*. Throughout the day, they used the *masa* to make fresh tortillas, patting it back and forth between their hands. The huge waterwheel also powered the electric saws that Emmanuel used to mill all of the timber for constructing houses across Tomendán.

For the next nine months, I worked with Emmanuel and Raoul, hoeing cane on the rocky slopes of Mt. Tepitario, planting corn and beans, harvesting mangoes that tasted like ambrosia, and enjoying tamales made from fresh corn. From the fields to the kitchen table, we talked for hours about our hopes, our dreams, and our fears. I quickly learned that the ejido faced many obstacles. All of the workers had different specialties, but nobody had mastery of the whole process. Hiring a maestro to oversee or consult on the operation was expensive. Organizing a collective effort was difficult, and each man's level of effort was different. This was especially true for the more exhausting roles, like keeping those hot ovens running. The work was never-ending, and the campesinos had a hard time selling their *piloncillos* for a good price. Making things worse, they covered their production costs by drawing credit from regional bureaucrats.

Long after my first encounter with the campesinos, I learned why they had been hesitant to bring me on. They were embarrassed to have me join them, Emmanuel explained. Embarrassed because the work they were doing was not sustaining them.

Knowing this now, I am amazed at how Raoul's and Emmanuel's families shared everything. We had fresh tortillas and beans with every meal, simple and perfect. We enjoyed many Mexican desserts made with *piloncillos*, the products of our hard work. My favorite desserts were *atole*, a sweet drink made from corn flour and seasoned with cinnamon and vanilla, and the ubiquitous flan. I learned to make *calabaza tachada*, an extraordinary dessert of winter squash. After cooking the calabaza squash in sugar-cane syrup overnight, we would collect it at dawn and pour fresh milk over the golden caramelized flesh of the squash. I was addicted for life after one bite of this local confection.

At family meals, I talked to my hosts about the problems facing the cooperative. Over many months, I came to understand that the ejido system that Emiliano Zapata had fought for in the Mexican Revolution was falling apart. Widespread corruption, illegal sales and transfers of ejido lands, ecological degradation, and low productivity were all contributing to the system's failure. The most heartbreaking thing of all was that the campesinos didn't trust one another. Drawing credit meant that profits were rarely realized. Where money was concerned, unity couldn't be built. The lack of trust was a difficult lesson to learn, a departure from the sense of solidarity I'd felt with the cause of Chilean farmers.

At length the conversations in Tomendán began to turn toward socialism and politics. For a while I held back my innermost thoughts, paranoid about being branded a Communist. Once, I worked up the courage to ask Emmanuel what the collective farmers in Tomendán thought about their prospects. His reply told me more than I was ready to hear.

"You know," he told me, "our problem here is how we treat each other. When one person begins to rise, he treats the rest of us as the patrón did in the time of the old hacienda. We have to learn. Our consciousness must grow."

I pondered the meaning of Emmanuel's words—what they meant for him and what his sentiment might mean for my own future in farming. Throughout my time in Tomendán, I had several other opportunities to reflect on the problems that the collective faced. I often attended the juntas (meetings) held by the campesino workers. We gathered in the old grain room of the hacienda, its doors thrown open. The older men sat in the corners, smoking cigarettes. The young men sat on wheelbarrows, on top of fertilizer bags, or on the unswept floor.

These meetings would practically swirl with changes in intensity. Sometimes there was laughing, sometimes yelling and finger-pointing. I remember one meeting where I was asked to take notes, because the elected secretary was hungover. There was a debate about the construction of a concrete basketball court, which had been bankrolled by a government commission in exchange for labor. It appeared that some of the men had pocketed their stipends without working on the project.

This kind of financial disagreement came up often. At one junta, a single member of the ejido spoke out and challenged the fragmentation of the group. Shouldn't we feel a sense of brotherhood, of common cause? It was easy for me to agree. But who was I to judge the conflicts in the lives of these *ejidatarios?* I had traveled to the village in order to learn about farming, but plenty of them would have gladly given it up if they'd had any choice.

When I returned to the States in the fall of 1974, I realized that it was my destiny to remain in my home country. I had made my second journey to Mexico without any timeline for a return, but the conflicts of the ejido had weakened my determination to remain outside the US. I think part of me also realized that I couldn't travel anywhere without bringing myself along. Probably I was ready to settle down. I had come a long way from Stanford, and I didn't feel like a kid anymore.

I don't think I could have put it into words back then, but in retrospect, I was clearly involved in a personal project of reshaping my family's legacy. I was consciously trying to distance myself from issues relating to the Vietnam War. Looking back, I am sure that the fact that there was no longer a draft contributed to my decision to return. I had no idea that the US's war would come to an end just months later, in April of 1975.

I felt at the time much as I had when Dad left the Pentagon; this could be another opportunity to turn a page in our family's life. Although I was deeply cynical about a US war planner weighing in on Latin American economic development, there were aspects of my father's work at the World Bank that I respected, especially his leadership in pushing the Bank to invest in global agriculture. I don't think he understood why I wanted to participate in agriculture at the level of the soil, but he understood on the most basic level that global agriculture was not meeting the needs of the globe.

In order to become a first-generation farmer in the United States, I needed an education. Not long after my second return, I hitchhiked from San Francisco to Davis. Acceptance letter in hand, I had decided to study agriculture. I reentered college as a twenty-five-year-old, and for the first time in my life, I was singularly focused on my education.

When I got to Davis, I did what most people do—I bought a used bike. My next job was to find a place to live. I knocked on dozens of doors, asking the unsuspecting occupants if they had a room to rent. Everyone said no. I think some of them had rooms available, but they took one look at me and shut the door. Finally, down by the train station, not fifty feet from the tracks, the door of a cottage opened and a woman appeared.

"Well, yes," she said, "my roommate just moved out. But I was looking for another woman."

Clearly I didn't fit the bill. Maybe retaining my hippie look—long hair, long beard—had something to do with my difficulties. I was so desperate that I blurted out, "I'm a good cook, and I do the dishes."

Mary Lou took me in. For the next year, I would be woken at 3 a.m. every day by the creaking and bumping of freight cars rolling past my window.

Farming is not an easy field for anyone. Even if you're passionate and educated, issues of land ownership and economics dictate whether you can make a living. I knew this even at the beginning of my studies. I felt innately that the next decade would be filled with peak stress. Remembering it now, everything from those days—the houses I lived in, my roommates, my regrets, the occasional visits from my parents—is encircled by the big narrative I'd defined for myself.

As a result, I think I took less notice of the ways in which the country was changing. Back in 1969, when I arrived at Stanford at the peak of the nation's unrest, there was a sense that a real widespread revolution of ideas was possible, maybe even imminent. Now, going into the mid-'70s, that momentum was winding down. The revolution hadn't arrived, but the national darkness that inspired it remained. It was a good thing that I saw a way forward in life through farming, because I think the national psyche was very damaged.

This was especially true for those who had returned home from fighting the war in Vietnam. Today we understand the decades-long aftereffects: veteran suicides in the thousands, posttraumatic stress, and a sense of national unity from the early 1960s replaced with absolute polarization. Back then I wasn't educated about these things and didn't allow myself to seek out any veterans or listen to the experiences of men who fought in the war. And I knew that they were around. Some of them were my peers.

For years I couldn't utter the word *Vietnam* without wanting to cry. There were many moments every day in which the subject of the war waded into my thought stream. It occupied the place of a childhood shame, early and overpowering. My horror concerning the war was never entirely absent from my experience; nor was it ever entirely present. In that way, the idea of the war was like my father, with whom I'd spent so much time yet whose absence I felt so acutely. Maybe I intentionally avoided the subject. The people in their late twenties who were my friends in Davis weren't eager to talk about it.

I graduated from UC Davis in December of 1976. Not long after receiving my diploma, I decided to look for some good soil. I hopped in my Datsun pickup truck and began a monthlong journey across America. The trip took me from Durango, Colorado, to Springfield, Ohio, and on to

Summertown, Tennessee. Along the way, I often paused by the side of country roads to take soil samples with an auger. Pressing the moist soil between my fingers, I would feel the mixture of sand, silt, and clay forming loam. With a sniff and a trained eye, I'd guess at the soil's organic matter percentage before taking my measurements.

While in Summertown, I stopped at something called The Farm, home to about three hundred hippies (spiritual seekers) who had caravanned from Haight-Ashbury. Their slogan: "Out to Save the World!"

This was a back-to-the-land community. Everyone grew food and adhered to strict vegan diets. To join, all you needed to do was sign a vow of poverty and turn over your cash and other possessions to the group. During my short stay on The Farm, I remember digging up huge orange yams with my hands. We pulled whole baskets of them from the red earth. The soil was good.

At the time, I thought of The Farm as a curious subculture. I can't remember how seriously I thought about joining that project. As I look back now on the entirety of my agricultural journey, my feelings about The Farm illustrate a transition in my thinking. The revolutionaries who inhabited The Farm seemed to be endeavoring to create a facsimile of the authentic subsistence farms I had encountered in South America. At one time it had been my dream and ambition to do something similar—maybe not in the United States, but certainly in Chile, with Carmen.

It struck me as I left The Farm that there was a significant political difference between the indigenous subsistence farmers who lived that life by necessity, by tradition, and by culture and the farmers who opted into it by renouncing their possessions. I felt that I could be more effective elsewhere. It was not that my politics had changed, but being in college in my midtwenties had definitely rounded the edges of my radicalism.

My relationship with Julie was a significant part of my thinking. She was from Jane Street in the West Village of New York City. She had come to UC Davis to work toward her master's in entomology and was one of the few women in the agriculture program. We met at an Aries party, a very Californian occasion that she still likes to joke about with her New York friends. I remember her being taken aback when she learned I was the son of Robert McNamara. She told me she had also been against the war. Julie understood that I wanted to be different from my father. Coming from New York, aware of the suffocating effects of East Coast society, she didn't judge me based on my family alone. To this day, Julie perceives people based on their integrity and trustworthiness rather than the success or failure of their parents.

After my visit to The Farm, I continued east, thinking about my family, my desire to start my own family, my political beliefs, my responsibilities, and everything I'd been through. There was a short visit with my folks in Washington. Like it or not, that was the first soil I grew in before I understood anything about actual soil. I wondered if the place where I had been planted was healthy. Certain things about it were. On that visit, I did not feel so alienated. The sight of refrigerators didn't make me have a panic attack as it had when I returned from Chile.

I was optimistic that things could get healthier and more natural between my father and me. I held out hope that, now that I was returning to the United States and settling down, we might start to have some of the honest conversations that I had wanted since I called him from the phone booth at St. Paul's. I didn't think I could fix what my father did or "save the world," like The Farmers. But I thought I could tell the truth about a violent legacy and try to do something better.

13.

Getting Home

After I graduated in 1976, I needed a way to break into the agriculture business as a first-generation farmer. In addition to traveling the country and visiting The Farm, I sought an agricultural apprenticeship. This was one approach to learning about the industry for non-landowners.

Dad sent many letters to his friends and colleagues, trying to help me get an apprenticeship. I don't think I was aware of Dad's letters at the time, but I recently discovered a large packet of them in my office. They always included my résumé. What strikes me about them is the sheer extent of Dad's network and his willingness to use it. He reached out to some of the nation's top agribusiness leaders, including Orville Freeman, who had served as secretary of agriculture when Dad was at Defense. From my childhood I remember evenings when Dad returned home with bruises up and down his legs from battles on the Pentagon squash court with Orville.

Although nothing came from these connections, reading

those letters now reminds me that Dad was behind me. At least, he was behind my career. He didn't have a clue how to address the turmoil he had caused me, but he was definitely willing to help my career.

Maybe I didn't remember these letters, or my dad's attempts to help me, for the same reason that a lot of our relationship is foggy: the shadow of him is just more powerful. It is mind-numbingly frustrating to know that he supported me—and to also know the extent to which he deprived me of understanding and of truth. I've sometimes worried that people will think I've ridden on his coattails. If they do feel that way, knowing the pain I felt from our underlying problems would probably do nothing to change their perception.

An early-morning swim with my father on South Beach, Martha's Vineyard,
circa 1974

*   *   *

My first venture after graduating from Davis was a truck-farming business. Julie and I rented a house in the hills above Winters, a hardworking agricultural community outside Sacramento with a colorful river flowing through its acres of shady orchards. I worked long hours planting, harvesting, and transporting a variety of crops on some rented farmland. These were long days that challenged our relationship and my own sanity. Truck-farming involves several yearly harvests and a lot of driving in order to deliver fresh produce to local markets. I was responsible for hiring numerous employees, managing multiple harvests, and running a roadside fruit stand. There was no guarantee after each season that the lease on my rented farmland would be renewed. This meant that I could be forced to move my business, myself, and my family at the end of each season. It soon became obvious that I couldn't sustain this lifestyle while also having the life I wanted. Julie and I both knew that we wanted a family, and I knew that I wanted to be a present and loving father.

When I began looking for a permanent farm to buy, it was during a seller's market. For over a year I drove down country roads in Yolo and Solano counties, looking for land for sale, without any luck. Driving the dusty lanes through almond and walnut orchards, I'd pull up to a farmer's home or headquarters and knock on their door.

I went back to one orchard a handful of times. It was owned by a Spaniard named Jose, who loved to tell stories. Over homemade *nocino*—walnut liqueur—he'd tell me tales of his youth in Almería. Every time I asked him about the possibility of buying his land, he'd serve me another shot of that sweet *nocino*. His nose would wrinkle, and he'd start telling a new tale. At last I realized that Jose just enjoyed these afternoon visits. A farmer never sells until he's broke, and Jose was far from broke.

Back when I was a student at UC Davis, I used to ride my bike along Putah Creek Road, which follows the creek from Davis to Winters. There was one piece of land that always caught my eye. Bordered by 40-foot-tall 120-year-old Mission olives, the chocolate-colored fields disappeared into the creek. The soil was rich and loamy, right in the heart of California's Mediterranean climate. Just glorious, as Dad would say.

Soon, I entered into negotiations with the owner of a walnut farm that bordered that land. I was drawn to the beauty of the walnut orchards, and I approached the weeks-long negotiations with the same intensity that my father must have harnessed when he met Henry Ford II. I had all my statistics written out on a yellow legal pad: the number of trees per acre; soil data; income and expense spreadsheets, and start-up costs—everything organized in columns.

I had youth on my side and the rough hands of a farmer to prove that I was genuine and ready to work. The owner of the walnut farm drove a hard bargain. He had been a top auto mechanic and restorer of classic cars in Sacramento before becoming a farmer. A year of farming, with broken irrigation pipes and broken dreams, had led him to sell. But he wasn't about to let his land go for a song. Channeling my father, I used my pencil and eraser to adjust my offer, inching it upward in large increments.

So close to achieving my dream, I could suddenly envision

myself as a walnut farmer. Walnuts fit all my criteria: they were sustainable and healthy, and I loved eating them. Walnuts are harvested only once a year; this fact would alleviate the pressures of multiple harvests that I felt in truck-farming. The beauty of the orchards and the nearby creek reminded me of the love I first felt in the land near the Patagonian fjords. I didn't consider the fact that I knew next to nothing about walnut agriculture.

During one of the pauses in our negotiations, I came home to Julie. I told her that I had fallen in love with the mechanic's farm and its walnut trees. She became quiet and thoughtful for a moment, and then she asked, "Is the farmhouse cute inside?"

"I haven't seen it," I told her.

I hadn't even asked to see the house. In my excitement to finally be bidding, I had never even considered how we would live. We were not married, but we were planning our future together. I had been thinking only of the land; I would have farmed and slept in a tent. Was this the sort of thing Dad might have done? He was always so focused on his career, and he didn't always acknowledge the people who supported him. This was the autumn of 1980. I was thirty years old, and I was rushing headlong into the rest of my life. As it turned out, the clapboard farmhouse consisted of a mudroom, a kitchen, three small bedrooms, and one bathroom.

August came around, and the days became scorching hot. Every drop of irrigation water disappeared into the soil, happy to escape the sun. I thought often of the shade provided by bigger walnut trees. We were nearing the end of the tug-of-war over the asking price for the farm. The owner said that he wanted to keep the proceeds from that year's harvest, coming up in October. More, he wanted to hold on to half of the mineral rights to the property. This meant he would have the right to extract oil and gas from beneath the surface of the soil should it ever be discovered. I had no intention of being a fossil fuel extractor, and this point of contention deeply frustrated me.

My cards were on the table. The edge of power and ego that Dad might have exerted in the same situation eluded me. In those days, I wished that I had the hardball stamina that he possessed. The owner sensed that I had nothing more to bargain with, and I caved to his demands. Years later, I'm glad I did. Had the mineral rights been a deal breaker, I wouldn't have gotten to farm this amazing piece of land.

Since we bought the place at the beginning of September, the pressure was on right away. In the art of walnut cultivation, the learning curve was vertical. I had about a month to plan for the harvest, facing the most difficult part of the business at the very beginning. One of my early adventures involved getting to know the land from the seat of my tractor, glimpsing my farm neighbors on their own vehicles in the low light of early mornings. As I drove the tractor, hawks exploded from the furrows in sudden flight. I remember, on one of the first days, stopping twice to lift an injured owl that I'd hit with the tractor, having tried so hard to miss him. I was quickly becoming obsessed with the beauty and sorrow of working that land.

The harvest lasted the full month of October, and the workdays were very long. As a beginning orchardist, I depended on the ideas and examples of my neighboring farmers. I wonder if they thought I was a bit of a pest. I was always asking them for advice. I often asked to rent or borrow equipment that I didn't yet own.

After hulling and drying the crop, I loaded the nuts into trailers and drove them into Winters for shelling and processing. This was a short trip, but it was scary as hell. After crossing the one-lane bridge over the creek, I had to swing the trailer, brimming with walnuts, hard to the left. There was a slight drop in the pavement right at the turn, which always caused the trailer to tilt precariously. I'd witnessed other walnut rigs tip over, spilling a million walnuts onto the pavement. I'd seen workers reloading the nuts with forklifts, shovels, and many hands. Carefully navigating the roads of my new community, I worried about what would happen if I lost money and time from an accident. I'd come a long way from the happy recklessness of climbing seaside cliffs on Rapa Nui.

That first season was a taste of the years to come. My dirty hands became more heavily calloused and my work boots quickly wore out. I was more exhausted than I had ever been, and I was happy.

That Thanksgiving, Julie and I had our first family celebration on the farm. Suffering from mesothelioma, wheelchair-bound and in enormous pain but with assistance from caretakers, my mom flew from DC to join us. She needed help at the gate, and when I first saw her in the chair, my eyes went to the ground for a moment. We all knew that she was going to die. Doctors had given her eleven months. I was mostly thinking about the pain she must be in.

At the farm, Mom rode the tractor with me through the

orchards. It must have taken a huge amount of willpower for her to allow me to hoist her up onto the metal seat. With a huff and a puff and a waft of diesel, the engine turned over, we lurched forward, and we were off and running together, one last time. Having lost all her hair, she wore a wig. The synthetic hair blew only slightly in the breeze as we rode, while the wind coaxed the walnut leaves from their limbs. We took a picture that captured her smile, miraculous in those days of sickness. Her determination to enjoy the visit was greater than her pain, greater than the fatigue caused by her many medications.

That evening, we had a small Thanksgiving dinner with family and friends. I don't remember any talk about my father. Why wasn't he there? I have no idea. The holiday was a time of celebration with my mother—of the farm, of the future life Julie and I would have. Mom and Dad would never be in Winters with us, together. Maybe it was denial of her sickness that kept him away. I know that he was immensely frustrated by the fact that she couldn't be cured. I ought to have insisted that he accompany her.

At the time, these questions needed no answers. We were focused on Mom, and on spending those days with her well. Julie and I were planning to get married and have a family. We knew Mom would never meet our children, and the emotions we felt must have filled in the big space left by Dad. He wasn't there with us, but the pattern felt normal.

I tried to make the most of Mom's last few months. I flew home for Christmas that year. I returned again to DC on January 16, 1981, to join Mom as she received the Medal of Freedom from President Carter at the White House. The President's remarks honored her work in literacy education.

It wasn't Dad who had pushed for Mom to receive the medal. My brother-in-law Bob Pastor had advocated for her, leveraging his position as a national security adviser. Dad already had his medal, from 1968. We attended the ceremony with her, and she remained in a wheelchair. I knew she didn't have long.

During the last weeks of her life, I dreamed of her often, and the dreams left me crying. We'd be meeting in the concourse of an airport. We were saying goodbye. She seemed aloof, which was so unlike her.

When the end seemed imminent, I returned to DC to say goodbye to her. She spent the last week of her life in our house on Tracy Place, in a hospital bed in the middle room of the second floor. Hospice workers attended to her, going in and out all day. I stayed in my old bedroom, the place where she'd comforted me as I sobbed over Fs on my homework assignments. From the second floor, now a thirty-one-year-old man, I overheard conversations Dad was having on the phone downstairs, calling all his friends in the medical field.

"Any possibility? Anything that might help Marg?"

Dad held out hope that a cure for Mom's disease would be discovered in time to save her. He spent a lot of time looking for that miracle and, I think, left her too much on her own. To hope is natural but to spend precious final days in a quixotic pursuit seems tragic to me now.

With Dad on the phone, I sat by Mom, next to her deathbed. I had thought her final gift to me was visiting the farm and seeing the beginning of my new life, leaving her impression in the soil even though she would never see what grew. That felt unbearably sad, but it wasn't the last gift after all. As she lay in her bed, she turned to me. Looking at me with her faded Pacific-blue eyes, she said, "Don't do as I have done. Don't give everything to others, so you have nothing left over for yourself."

Those words were shattering. Throughout my life, I had always tried to model my existence after her role as the giver. She had just received the nation's highest civilian honor for her service.

She told me again, "Just remember to give to yourself."

I realized then how hard it was going to be to live in this world as my father's son without her.

The first time Dad visited the farm was for our wedding in 1982. Other than his presence, he didn't contribute much to the ceremony. For me, it was a wonderful event with a streak of pain because Mom's death was still so recent. For Julie, I think there was a mixture of joy and discomfort. During our UC Davis days, she had spent time with my father when my parents visited, but our wedding was the first time her parents had ever met him. She recalls being seated between our two dads at the dinner table. Her father, Jim, was an Irish cop and restaurateur from Brooklyn. Known as Big Jim or Diamond Jim, he had a larger-than-life personality, which evidently paired interestingly with my father's. Julie has several stories about the encounter. One of them involves Dad asking Big Jim if he had ever been backpacking in Yosemite.

"I've never been to Yos-uh-might," Jim replied. He

added that the only time he went backpacking was between steakhouses, with a few beers in his bag. Later, and
with a good dose of humor, Julie nicknamed my dad "Big
Mac."

Julie's is a family of singers and joke tellers, and everyone
has a nickname. This was never the case for the McNamaras.
Our marriage was the beginning of an evolution for me
in my perception of my family and its dysfunction—out
of the familiar dark, again. I also can't overlook the pain
that Julie has felt in coming to grips with being part of
my family. I know that she felt marginalized by my father
at times. I also know that she was continually hurt by his
absence from the farm, from our lives, and from her life
more specifically. Dad supported our choices, but he placed
a boundary around his personal life, which almost seemed
like a condition of his financial support. Though officially
retired, he kept himself busy. After Mom's death, he was on
numerous corporate boards, and he began writing books. He
threw himself into these things, I think, in order to cope with
losing Mom.

Soon his grandchildren were growing in the California
sunshine, the same sunshine that nurtured him as a young
man. Our oldest son, Graham, was born in September of
1984, just as the walnut harvest was getting underway. In the
delivery room, the nurses weren't sure if I should touch my
baby son, because my hands were so stained from walnuts.
I often took Graham with me on the farm as we harvested
the crop. For Julie and me, new parents, he was the center
of our world, and we enjoyed introducing him to all of our
friends.

I don't think Dad was aware of how much we missed him. I

had often hoped that being a grandfather would help ease the regrets of his life and the loss of Mom, but his pattern of absence continued. It was another missed opportunity to come closer together as a family. Instead, he called on the phone to talk about the production of the farm—or when he needed help. Being a lifelong incompetent at household tasks, and with Mom no longer around, Dad used to call Julie and have her recite instructions about operating the washing machine, the dishwasher, or the coffee maker, writing everything down while she spoke into the phone.

There was another factor adding to the pain in our family life. Dad was my financial partner.

I couldn't have afforded to purchase farmland on my own. Throughout my life, Mom and Dad had set aside savings for my sisters and me. My savings went toward the down payment we made on the farm and our house.

That had always been part of the plan; I had anticipated borrowing from my parents when I had my own farming business. The goal was to eventually buy out Dad's shares in our operation and be independent, but I knew that we faced a long road to get there. Work and ingenuity alone wouldn't be enough; we were also beholden to the climate and global prices, plus local politics and economics. I remember those first two years, both buying the farm and getting married, as filled with tremendous pressure compounded with a sense of risk. Although my father had put me in a position to achieve my dream, my thoughts and feelings toward him were still conflicted. I was mostly attuned to the self-conscious feeling of being in debt—owing money, making payments.

Julie's position made things more complicated at home. We lived on the farm together for two years before we were married. Because Dad and I were legal partners prior to our marriage and since the farm borrowed heavily on its annual production loan, Julie had to sign a quitclaim deed issued by our lender each year. In doing so, she transferred any interest that she had in the property to my father and to me, thereby quitting any right or claim she had. Every year until we paid off the loan, as the date to sign the quit-claim approached, I shuddered, lost sleep, and felt sadness and anger. It caused such heartache between Julie and me. It was not right that she was being forced by the bank to sign a loan document that was neither fair nor necessary. It was also not something I had much say in. It was one of those intractable problems in a relationship, the type of thing that my family never talked about. Had my mother and father gone through something similar, it probably would have been painted over with the words *We never had any problems.*

"Your family isn't normal," Julie sometimes told me. Without her perspective, I doubt I would have learned to see them with some distance and objectivity.

Dad never understood the nuts and bolts of the farm. I could tell that he appreciated my love for the work, but he truly didn't know a thing about production agriculture. Sometimes when we talked on the phone, all he wanted was big data. His constant requests for spreadsheets, financial balances, and rate of return bothered me. In fact, those conversations reminded me of the misleading statistics that had so doomed his wartime strategy.

I remember him saying that he couldn't taste the difference between organic ingredients and something produced conventionally. Coming from a person who liked to drink freeze-dried Sanka coffee, who insisted that it tasted the same as a freshly brewed pot, I kind of believed him. But he was also a lover of garden-fresh tomatoes. My earliest memories are of him and my mother in their garden in Ann Arbor, plucking the juiciest red tomatoes from their vines. With a saltshaker in one hand, he'd sprinkle salt on the red, ripe flesh in the other and take a huge bite, the tangy juice, seeds, and shiny tomato skin dribbling down his chin, landing on his khaki shirt.

"Boy, this is a great tomato," he'd say.

As an adult, when I tried to explain to Dad that organic produce really does have a richer, fuller flavor, I used tomatoes to illustrate my point. Also statistics.

"You see, Dad," I tried to say once, "a tomato is ninety-three to ninety-six percent water…"

And, I went on to say, the quality and mineral content of the soil and the climate in which a tomato is grown really do contribute to the flavor. This combination of factors is referred to as terroir. That would have been during one of our many phone calls when we discussed the business and finances of the farm.

The 7:45 a.m. phone calls might be the thing I remember most about our partnership. That's 7:45 a.m. East Coast time, 4:45 a.m. in California. Dad's rationale for calling before 8 a.m. was cost savings, as the rates went up after eight o'clock. He was a true Scotsman, thrifty and efficient. It would be pitch-black outside, and the phone by my bed would ring. Julie still says that she'd have to "peel me off the ceiling" as I grabbed the phone.

On the other end of the line, with an inquisitive voice, my father would ask, "How's the walnut crop looking, Craigie?"

"Dad, I can't really see the crop. It's still dark."

His questions would roll from the phone like a cascading river: Is there enough labor? Have you considered vertically integrating your business? How's the market? With the sun not yet up, just that first glow on the horizon, I'd think back to faded black-and-white images of him sitting before some congressional committee, getting grilled, until he'd jolt me to awareness with another sharp query.

Eventually I'd make it down to the kitchen. There I was at least able to get a cup of tea while talking to him. As quickly as the call began, it would end. It was 7:59, and the rates were going up.

I was totally oriented toward sustainability, which was an unusual attitude in the 1970s. I'm not sure I ever convinced Dad that organic produce tastes better. I do know that he enjoyed eating our organic walnuts, especially on cross-country ski trips to the hut we had built in memory of Mom along the Continental Divide. As long as I was carrying the extra weight of the nuts in my backpack, he was all in. Our lunch spot on those trips, the one we had picked out twenty years prior, was alongside a fallen aspen tree. We'd need to brush off a foot of new snow from its trunk in order to set our backpacks down and spread out lunch. When we sat down and he saw the lunch ingredients emerge, I could tell he appreciated me for carrying his food, which was the heaviest addition to the pack. He liked to have a slab of Vermont cheddar cheese on whole wheat with a slice of tomato. For dessert he liked Toblerone Swiss Milk Chocolate with honey and nougat.

"Only two triangular pieces, please."

Our ongoing ski trips provided material for conversations. He was so loving during those times, and the walnuts I'd grown were in his hands. We had a bond with nature that came from the beauty of those surroundings. But that did not replace the missing pieces. Eating walnuts with him on the trail reminded me that he had not visited the orchards for a very long time.

"When do you think you might get out again, Dad?"

"I'm not sure, Craigie. How's it looking?"

We had perfected the paradox of our relationship. We were so close on trips to the mountains, and his absence wounded me deeply during all the other times. Each hiking or skiing trip repaired the hurt a little, and then the emotional scabs would break open.

My love for Dad contributed to what was a kind of identity crisis. When I was a young walnut farmer, my dreams were coming true: a beautiful new family, something I'd always wanted. However, I was now a landowner—a *momio*. I still felt strongly aligned with socialist politics. I still admired Fidel Castro. In the beginning of my farming career, I truly believed that making a profit was wrong. This was juxtaposed with Dad's more industrial approach. It was not a comfortable time. I talked in the early mornings with my father, who had loaned me money, who had been in LBJ's cabinet, and he always asked me about the goddamn spreadsheets.

Farming over many decades made me aware of qualities in myself that come from my father: a desire to work, far-reaching ambition, and a drive to push forward through every obstacle. It was not easy to be his partner or his son, but in this part of my life, I truly discovered myself as both.

As I was remembering this time, I became interested in doing something Dad might have done. I analyzed my income. I opened my most recent annual report from Social Security and followed my number from the first year I started to earn a salary. In 1967, at seventeen years of age, I earned $260. There were several years while I was on the road in Latin America when I earned zero.

Things picked up a bit when I drove a tractor during tomato harvest in the summer of 1977. I earned $6,170 that year. The year I bought our farm, 1980, I earned $28,197. For the next twenty-five years, my salary hovered around $50,000.

First-generation farmers are rare. The pressures and risks defeat many people. The entry price deters others or keeps them out of the game. I know that I had help, but I also never thought of my career as something belonging to me alone. It was about the land and the crop, the substance of what I was doing. My responsibility, I felt, was to deliver a healthy and sustainable product.

To Dad it was more of a business. I wish he had come and walked the orchards with me, dug the soil with me, held it in his hands. I remember his hands as smooth, his fingers long and narrow. Those hands were more accustomed to holding pencils than nails. He always tracked and calculated the elevation of his daily ski runs. At the end of each day, with gusto and a happy sense of accomplishment, he would announce how many vertical feet he had skied that day. Over the course of many summers hiking the Rockies or walking briskly on South Beach at Martha's Vineyard, his arms and legs became freckled and tan. But he didn't know about toiling with the earth.

14.

Back Pages

I've kept a journal for most of my adult life. On the shelves to the left of my computer, below an indoor beehive, I have many volumes of binders. Each volume begins with a prologue, addressed to my family.

I've not tried to couch in gentle language the events or emotions that I've experienced. Rather I've written about them as they occurred, expressing both joy and pain of the moment.

The ratio of joy to pain changes from year to year. During my first stint in college, at Stanford, there was an abundance of pain and less joy. Back then I wrote in many notebooks, poems and love letters and stray thoughts and momentary rages. I still have the logbook from the first Mexico road trip with Will and Rob. There are pictures inspired by our travels, and there are entries in which we berate the world, often in jest, because we were suffering from bug bites and stomachaches and heat.

Fuck you, log, you piece of shit.

Do you have to eat rice and beans until it's coming out of your ears?

Do you have to drive a heavy motorcycle over some of the worst roads in creation—at night, in the rain?

Do you have to take your malaria pills without water?

Do you get devoured by insects?

We'll see who makes it to Tierra del Fuego.

There are thousands of pictures from Rapa Nui in my journals, adding color to the hundreds of pages documenting my island life. Not long ago, I opened one of these notebooks and turned to one of the last entries I made. I came across the phrase *my heart is weeping*. I wrote that because my friend had passed away. Maria. She was part of Vera's extended family, the one who introduced me to a new community on Easter Island. She was the whole reason I got to go there, and she died on March 22, 1973, from tuberculosis. We had so little language between us, a great cultural distance, and yet she was someone for whom I felt great love, uncomplicated by any awareness of difference. What did I do for her? I know I appreciated her. Was it enough?

I kept a journal when I worked on the ejido in Tomendán, even more extensive than my scribblings from Rapa Nui. Much of my writing was about the life and the atmosphere of that place. I wrote about how the breeze tugged on the curtains of Raoul's home in Tomendán.

The two brothers I met in Tomendán, Raoul and Emmanuel, had families with three and eight children. They cooked over wood-fire hearths. Life without running water or electricity made for long days of gathering firewood, collecting water, and sweeping the earthen floors with ash from the fire to sanitize them. And the ejido faced many obstacles. Raoul once told me, "We are like slaves of the government," because the local administrators endeavored to trap them in debts they could never get out of, no matter how much sugar cane they refined.

An early page from my Tomendán journals alludes to an undercurrent of violence in that community:

I accompanied the family to a little movie theater in the town. It was like a wooden barn, with a crowd of people gathered around waiting for the shows to start. While we milled about, eating and drinking, we talked about a man who was shot a few days ago.

It had been a drunken argument, and the police didn't apprehend the murderer, who ran into the countryside. Later I learned about the volume of political killings in the area. If a low-level campesino got too involved in politics, there was a good probability that the local power brokers would put a hit out on him. Walking to the fields in the early morning by the free-flowing stream through that town, feeling the wind before the heat of the day came, I found it difficult to imagine such violence. To my eyes, Tomendán was another paradise: good work, good food, a banana and mango tree here and there. Comparing my notes from that time with my notes from Rapa Nui, I ask myself if I was attempting to re-create one experience in another.

*I have tried not to see Tomendán and its people through my
often romantic and naive viewpoint. I am unsure if I've fulfilled
this or not.*

In the ensuing decades I would return to Tomendán every
four years. First, I brought my friends Will and Kate. Later, I
brought my young sons, Graham and Sean. We helped Emmanuel build a greenhouse to grow cucumbers. I felt grateful
that my boys got to suck the sweet juice from sugar cane
that they harvested with machetes, enjoy fresh tamales, pick
mangoes and let the juice run down their chins, ride burros,
and live without running water and electricity—all as I had
done while living with Emmanuel and Lola long before the
boys were born.

Many years later, on a mild March afternoon in 1997, I
got a phone call. An unfamiliar voice introduced himself in
Spanish. This person—I'll call him Pedro—said that he was
from Taretan, a town I knew well just a few kilometers from
Tomendán. He told me that he had fallen in love with Lupe,
the daughter of Juan, a friend of mine from the village with
whom I'd worked hoeing sugar cane. The couple had decided
to elope and travel to El Norte.

I first met Lupe when she was only three years old.
Searching my memories, I recalled our hikes to the *cascadas*,
the waterfalls, where she'd run behind her brothers on the
dusty path leading up to the three falls. She had enormous
and lovely brown eyes.

On the phone, Pedro told me that he had paid a coyote
to get them across the border. They were in a sleepy cantina
now on the US side. From the jukebox in the background, I

could hear one of my favorite *rancheras* melodically describing Mexican life. Meanwhile Pedro explained that he had worked very hard over a two-year period to raise $1,200, which they had given to the coyote. Now that they had crossed the border, he said, the coyote was demanding $1,500 more.

I took a deep breath. I told Pedro that I needed to make a call to Tomendán to verify the story. I knew the owner of the *panadería*, the bread shop, where the town phone was located. I called up the bakery owner, Dona Luisa. I asked her in Spanish if she could possibly run up to the shop and put my friend Juan on the line.

Soon, I heard his voice. "Roberto, *como estas?*"

Craig is difficult to pronounce in Spanish, so I am known as Roberto to my friends in Tomendán.

After asking about Juan's wife, their children, and the sugar-cane harvest, I asked if it was true that Lupe had eloped. With a sigh, he said, "*Si.*"

That was all I needed to know. I thanked him and said that I would call back later. With some trepidation, I dialed the number of the border cantina again. The phone was passed to Pedro, and the rest of the story unfolded quickly. The coyote had threatened to rape Lupe and kill Pedro if they didn't pay up immediately.

I could feel tightness in my throat, and I sensed Pedro's fear. He continued to talk, but I interrupted him and asked to speak to the coyote. This man was just as I had imagined: threatening, full of machismo, wicked, and mean. He demanded his *pago*. My fingers gripped the receiver tightly, pressing it closer to my ear. When I couldn't stand it any longer, I screamed into the phone in Spanish, "Shut up, you lazy son of a bitch." I told him that if he touched them, I'd string him up by his balls for the real coyotes to feast on.

After a few minutes of yelling at each other, he told me that if I wired him the money via Western Union, he would let them go. Without hesitation, I jumped into my pickup truck and drove to our local Town and Country Market. I'd never sent a Western Union wire before. But many of my farm employees used this service, because most of them had families in Mexico, in towns like Tomendán and Taretan.

I sent the money. By the time I returned to my office, Pedro and Lupe were back on the road again, away from the coyote. Later I was able to call Juan and let him know that the situation had been resolved. I know that the couple eventually made it to California.

It was a horrifying event, but I knew it happened all the time because of America's broken immigration system. I asked myself if I was doing enough to run a fair-farming business, and if there was more I could do, at least on the local level, to address the unfairness of the overall system. On the other hand, I realized that my actions could have unintended consequences. Helping undocumented immigrants cross the border might preclude me from certain leadership opportunities. Certainly I could never serve as secretary of agriculture after that; somebody would find out. Couldn't I do more to help by having a position with influence?

These thoughts came from Dad. I suppose my fantasies about serving in a cabinet also related to him. I'm glad that I sent that money. I would have done the same thing to help my own kids, or Will's kids. It concerned my friends.

*   *   *

While I've thought of myself as a political radical, I had a friend on Rapa Nui who was a true radical. I wrote about her in my journal—ten days into my island life.

Her name was Louisa. I don't remember how we met. In my journal, I wrote:

> *Her homeland is Austria. Her life has been the struggle of the proletariat. She is a Jew, a Russian, and a German, and she is in Chile to support Allende and make revolution.*

She was visiting Rapa Nui to take a break from her organizing work in Santiago. By this time, I was well known as the local milkman.

Louisa told me stories, fabulous tales, some invented, some real, and all magical. They seemed to me like fantasies of far-off lands. Europe, where she'd come from, seemed as exotic as the Pacific island I'd been calling home. She had stories about traveling with Jimi Hendrix. There were too many stories to list.

Her real focus was work. After ten days, she left Rapa Nui as mysteriously as she had arrived, and we never saw each other again. For years, we stayed in touch through letters. Hers were typed on rice paper. Often she would add cursive in the margins of her long, typed sentences. The letters told of the dystopia that Santiago was becoming.

> *Yesterday a member of the communist party here in the village told me: We recognize you as a revolutionary. We will defend you, whatever is going to happen.*

Much later, after I returned to the States, Louisa's correspondence continued to arrive at 2412 Tracy Place in Washington. One letter, dated November 10, 1973 — exactly sixty days after the assassination of Allende — reads as follows:

Dear Craig,

Thanks for your letter from the 12th of September. Don't send stuff like that to me anymore. Censorship. I'll leave for Europe at the end of November, not sure, maybe later.

We have got some plans and we need your help. We need contacts and unfortunately bread. We need technical equipment, for example that tiny Japanese camera in order to shoot pictures without arousing suspicion. We are creating an underground information center. That is all I can tell you. Don't use the correo.

See you — L

When I read that letter now, I see the irony in the fact that it arrived at the home of the former US secretary of defense, whose son sent money to the person who wrote that letter so she could buy bread. The father in that house designed a war against Communism in Vietnam, and the son supported a person fighting a war on the side of socialism in Chile.

A year later, Louisa was back in Europe, where she helped Chilean refugees who had fled the Pinochet regime. She still wrote to me, and I still have her letters. They're tucked into my journals, loose and toward the back.

One of the letters I wrote to Louisa contained a story about my father: he used to walk the length of the Vietnam Memorial at night, a shadow in the dark, somehow going unrecognized. Like that image, which comes from a place I can't remember, Louisa's words exist in a place beyond conversation, deeper than happiness, less tangible than the soil of my orchards but even more a part of the soil in which I grow.

Am I a revolutionary? Do I really fulfill my duties, my respon-sibilities? Do I work hard enough? Am I doing enough?
   My eyes are tired. So long, be good. Venceremos.

PART 3

15.

Telluride

The place where my father and I came closest to a true meeting of minds was not Washington. Nor was it Martha's Vineyard, nor Colorado, nor Vietnam itself. It was the Telluride Film Festival.

When I was a kid, our family visited Colorado for ski vacations every winter, and I always wanted to check out Telluride. Long before the launch of the festival in the mid-1970s, in the days when I struggled to keep up with my father in the mountains, I can remember wanting to ski the slopes there.

When the opportunity to go to the film festival presented itself in 2003, it came as an invitation from Dad. I remember the day he called to say that *The Fog of War,* a film about him by the documentarian Errol Morris, was headlining Telluride. At eighty-seven, he spoke in a voice with a gravelly texture and lilt, left in his throat by an esophageal diverticulum.

"Dad," I said, "are you sure you want me there?"

For a moment I was transformed back into his young son,

looking up to him with stars in my eyes, on the way to a lunch visit at LBJ's White House. Here was a chance to be close to a kind of spotlight. I wasn't overly familiar with Errol Morris's work, but his reputation was enormous. There was also some trepidation. I anticipated the confrontations—with the past, with my father's detractors—that Errol's film might force.

There had been occasions prior to 2003 when I wanted an invitation from Dad, and they never came. One example was his reconciliation trip to Cuba in 1992, which included a meeting with Fidel Castro to mark the fiftieth anniversary of the Cuban Missile Crisis. Aside from my admiration for Castro, I felt that it was my right to attend this event. It made sense for me to be with Dad to reflect on his role in bringing the world to the brink of Armageddon. But he wanted to go it alone. Only he wasn't really alone. My brother-in-law Bob Pastor accompanied him on the trip. Later, speaking with Bob, I learned that he felt at times marginalized and put down by my father, though he wouldn't say exactly what Dad did or said to him. Maybe it's good that I didn't go to Cuba. Maybe Dad didn't think a dirt-covered walnut farmer ought to be in the room with all those distinguished statesmen.

Talking with Dad over the phone, probably looking at my calendar to see if it was possible to squeeze in the visit and leave the orchards behind, I sensed in his voice a need to have me with him in Telluride. This was not a political event where he would be surrounded by the trappings of government and leadership. This was a chance for the culture at large to form a new judgment. It was a vulnerable position for him; he'd be even more exposed than in the pages of his memoir.

In the weeks leading up to the festival, he called me

more than he usually did. I think he was anxious; he did not have any editorial control over the film and didn't know how it would portray him. Throughout his career, he had weathered criticism, but it had always been from a position of power—as head of Defense, head of the World Bank, or as a respected member on one of his various boards. The very title *The Fog of War* described uncertainty and called into doubt his reputation as the ultracompetent manager.

On the morning I traveled, he called the farm around 6 a.m., when I was already on my way to the airport. He called me on my cell around 4 p.m., to see if I had arrived in Colorado. I couldn't remember the last time he was so eager to see me.

I arrived during a Rocky Mountain thunderstorm. As I got off the plane and walked by the big windows of the airport, an evening rainbow formed over the city. It was Labor Day weekend 2003, and it was a glorious evening. I drove a rental car from the airport to Telluride. The drive through the mountains took me past some beautiful vistas and around some big curves, and I drove fast, full of anticipation and excitement. I was reminded of the feelings I had as a child or teenager when Dad wanted me to go hiking or skiing with him.

My hotel room downtown included a bag of swag, with a comfy fleece vest and some thumb drives, which were novel in 2003. This was sort of exciting to me. I felt that I'd arrived at an important event where I had a backstage pass. Dad was staying in the same hotel, a few rooms away. He was with his girlfriend, who later became his second wife.

The three of us walked to a nearby restaurant and took an

intimate corner table. It was a time to catch up. Over dinner Dad was unusually talkative, in a very good mood. He wanted me to update him on the farm and to talk about the kids. We chatted a little about *The Fog of War,* and I could tell he was nervous. He and I both remembered the huge blowback from *In Retrospect.*

"It's good to have you here, Craigie," he told me. He knew I loved him.

After the meal, he retired to his hotel room to rest up for what lay ahead: press interviews, meetings with Errol and Sony Productions, and a banquet after the screening. Before I turned in for the night, I watched *Elephant,* a drama written and directed by Gus Van Sant. Loosely based on the Columbine High School massacre, *Elephant* left me dazed. I had a restless sleep, with dreams of national tragedies.

The next morning, as we got ready for the screening in our separate hotel rooms, I imagined that Dad and I were both wondering how the press and the glitterati would perceive him. The Rockies had always been a place where we were on common ground. I carried his belongings and food on my back; he taught me how to make a fire. We cooked our meals together over a blaze as the mountain glow closed our evenings. We were quiet for hours on the trail, and I could predict exactly what he would say when we made our first rest stop at Snowmass Lake or Van Horn Park. We shared stories of our love for my mother, and we shared the beauty of Mother Nature.

Now here we were, in the Rockies again, surrounded by devoted movie lovers and filmmakers, people very different from us. For all his fame and infamy and all it brought me, compared with the glamour of the movies, the two of us were quite ordinary people. Surely we could share in that feeling.

Yet he was absent again. After our dinner on the first night, I didn't speak to him for the next twenty-four hours. This pattern more or less continued for the entire duration of the festival. I'm not sure why he decided to exclude me after the first night, or if it was even conscious. My best guess is that he felt himself at the center of his own story during the festival. I was a supporting player, to be called upon only if needed. He wanted to receive any praise that would come, and he wanted to absorb any of the pain. For a person who had always been so singularly driven, ambitious, and self-centered, the distinction between the positive and negative effects of all this attention might not have been very clear. My father took the opposite approach to mine on the farm, where I always wanted to have my team around me and make everyone feel included.

In any case, I was left to enjoy my time alone. And I took advantage of it. Shit, I was fifty-three years old; it's not like I was lonely or couldn't find something to do. I hiked up to Bridal Veil Falls and watched as clear Colorado spring water plunged 365 feet down into the Telluride valley. I sat alone in a dark theater, mesmerized by *The General*, the 1926 silent comedy starring Buster Keaton.

It just wasn't with my dad. There was no invitation to join him at any of the press events or the special dinners or private conversations.

*   *   *

I stood in line with more than five hundred guests to see *The Fog of War*, a deep sense of isolation and aloneness overwhelming me. I was waiting to watch a story that I had no control over, even if I knew how it ended. I was there only to see how the story would be told.

In the theater, Ken Burns was sitting to my right and up one row. Alice Waters sat to my left. Close to the stage was a figure whose name I wouldn't know for another twelve years, an aspiring filmmaker, nativist, and future global disrupter: Stephen K. Bannon.

After the film, I was invited to dinner with a handful of journalists and film aficionados. Dad and Errol Morris attended a different dinner. I didn't see them before, during, or after the screening.

The restaurant was dark. The table was long. The group was about eight. Normally I'm quite extroverted at meals. That night, I was quiet. I looked often at my plate and at the silverware. I can't remember what I ordered. I remember adjusting my position a lot, shifting in my seat in a sheltering posture.

There were some positive comments during dinner. The reception of the film was good. The reception of my father was also positive, but in a more complicated way. I recall some conversation and mild debate about whether he deserved credit for opening up all these years later.

Across the candlelit table from me was a man about my age. I didn't know him, and we hadn't spoken to each other. I noticed, as we ate the main course, that he was having a rather quiet side conversation with his dinner partner. When I looked at him, there were knives coming out of his eyes. As dinner was drawing to an end, I started to have the lonely feeling of being cornered.

As everyone was getting ready to leave, the man across from me stood up and turned to face me. In no uncertain terms, he let me know that he hated my father; no, he *despised* him for being an unredeemable war criminal. *Pure evil.* That's what he said.

I don't remember how I responded. It was not a big confrontation, and I'm not the type of person who makes a scene in a restaurant. What I remember most is leaving the place, deeply wounded, and lying awake in my hotel bed that night, chastising myself. *What did you expect to find here? Fucking closure?*

Maybe my antagonist and I could have had a conversation. Perhaps his brother's name or his father's name was etched in the Vietnam Veterans Memorial wall. Did he once walk the dark shadows of the black granite, reflecting on a loss that ravaged his heart?

I would have listened to him. I would have sided with him. I would have said, *Look, I protested—I went to the induction center—I left the country—I hung the damn Stars and Stripes upside down in my bedroom. I did what I could. Maybe I could have done more—but there it is.* Perhaps, through a conversation like that, we might have empathized with each other. We might have sat for an hour, agreeing with each other in increasing volume, feeling increasing shared anger.

But that man didn't want this. That night, all he wanted was to hurt me. He wanted to let anyone near Robert McNamara know his pain. Maybe it was something he needed to get off his chest. I could understand that. I've harbored the same feelings.

*　　*　　*

Several months passed between the screening at Telluride and a follow-up event at UC Berkeley. Mark Danner, then a professor at the Berkeley graduate school of journalism, was going to interview Errol Morris and my father at Zellerbach Hall on the Berkeley campus. Dad hadn't been back to Cal for decades. The last time was most likely at the beginning of the war, when the campus was the epicenter of the antiwar movement.

Julie and our three children piled into the car, and we drove down to Berkeley from Winters. Prior to the interview, we attended a reception for my father at the University House, formerly the president's mansion and now the home of the chancellor. When Dad was a student at Cal, he dated Marion Sproul Goodin, the daughter of Robert Gordon Sproul, president of the University of California system from 1930 to 1958. Nearly every UC campus has a Sproul Hall. UC Berkeley has Sproul Plaza, the site of numerous demonstrations and rallies over the years. Marion grew up in this Mediterranean-style villa at the heart of the campus. I can only imagine the memories Dad must have experienced in that house. Perhaps he thought back to a time when he was full of potential: a young kid growing up in the Depression era, attending college and with an uncertain future.

As we walked with my father from the University House to the auditorium, passing the assembled crowd, my mind went into frenzy mode. There were several hundred people outside, and we were told that the theater was filled to capacity—about twenty-seven hundred people. I was envisioning the antiwar demonstrations that I had participated in on the Berkeley campus—police in full riot gear with loaded shotguns pointed at us, and tear gas leaving a haze over the campus. I remembered police cars screaming up the avenues, missing us by inches. Had Bob McNamara spoken on campus in 1969, Berkeley would have been on fire.

I wondered how many people attending *The Fog of War* interview were with me on those marches. In that moment, I was thinking not about Dad's mistakes as the former secretary of defense but only about his safety. He was my father, and I was afraid that he would be attacked, during or after the interview. I didn't want his grandchildren to see that happen.

We sat in the front row. My kids were on either side of me. As crazy as it seems, I was prepared to climb up on the stage and tackle anyone who came near him. I wasn't in the same condition that I'd been in as the MVP of my high school football team, but I'd been farming for the past quarter century. I felt I was strong enough.

When Dad came out onstage, the auditorium fell silent. The possibility of confrontation—the awkwardness and the silent threat—was in the air like electricity before a thunderstorm.

The moderator showed selected clips from *The Fog of War*. The clips focused on my father's "Eleven Lessons," first enumerated in his memoir, *In Retrospect*, and later used by Errol Morris as a through line for the film. The lessons are:

1. Empathize with your enemy.
2. Rationality alone will not save us.
3. There's something beyond one's self.
4. Maximize efficiency.
5. Proportionality should be a guideline in war.
6. Get the data.
7. Belief and seeing are both often wrong.

8. Be prepared to reexamine your reasoning.
9. In order to do good, you may have to engage in evil.
10. Never say never.
11. You can't change human nature.

During the conversation that followed, Mark Danner pushed my father on these lessons, attempting to draw out a comparison with Iraq. At one point, Danner asked specifically whether the lessons from the Vietnam War should be applied to America's impending adventure in 2003. My father steadfastly refused to comment. He gave various reasons—among them that it could pose a risk to American soldiers in the field. He also said that ex-cabinet members shouldn't comment on the jobs current cabinet members are doing. He would repeat these nonanswers to the Iraq question in numerous other interviews.

For those of us who despised Dick Cheney and Donald Rumsfeld and felt the invasion of Iraq was a mistake, it was frustrating that Robert McNamara wouldn't comment directly. It brought back painful memories of his silence after 1968. There had been such hope and such disappointment.

"We human beings killed a hundred and sixty million other human beings in the twentieth century," he said. He was almost shouting, jabbing his finger at Mark Danner. "Is that what we want in this century?"

In classic fashion, Dad answered his own question. "I don't think so!"

At one point, Danner asked Dad how he dealt with reporters during difficult press conferences as secretary of defense. Dad said, "Don't answer the question they asked. Answer the question you wish they'd asked."

Does this mean tell a lie? Growing up in his house, with his rules, I considered him to be an honest person. I'm sure I can remember him saying "Don't tell lies" when I was a little kid. I'm sure that I passed on to my own children the same lesson. How could someone as intelligent as Dad fail to see the contradiction?

Maybe his hypocrisy has to do with Lesson Number Three. That's the one that matters most to me. I think it's the one he most failed to live up to.

As the interview was winding down, and after encouraging the audience to read his book *In Retrospect*, Dad said, "I'm not suggesting you buy it—but the lessons are in there. I put them forward not because of Vietnam; I put them forward because of the future."

When Dad felt like he was done with an interview, he was done. In true Bob McNamara style, he packed up his briefcase mid-question, before Danner called the conversation off. To this day, with some embarrassment and amazement, my children remember him heading offstage without answering the last question, to thunderous applause.

After the event, Alice Waters invited Mark Danner, Errol Morris, my father, and my family to a private dinner at Chez Panisse. To the best of my knowledge, this was the first time that Waters and my father had met. It certainly was the first time that I had met her. Many years later, she told me that when she shook my father's hand, he reached out to her and put a walnut from our orchards into her palm. Her reaction then was the same one I had when she told me the story: amazement, surprise. That simple gesture was a sign of peace, a desire for a healthy future, and his love for me.

*   *   *

Having yearned throughout my adult life for a conversation with Dad about his role in history, I'm fascinated by Errol Morris's experiences interviewing him for twenty-three hours.

Errol shot his film using a machine he invented called the interrotron, which allows the director and the subject to talk to each other through the camera lens, creating an eye-to-eye interview, something Errol terms "first-person cinema." The technique creates an unnerving intimacy, similar to being at a therapy session or in a confessional booth.

I once asked Errol what it was like to spend so much time with my father. He responded that he felt my father was thoughtful and self-doubting: a decent and magnificent man, a person he deeply respected and learned a lot from. He liked him. However, he also told me that he felt conflicted about the decisions my father made as secretary of defense. He said that he considered Dad a war criminal. I wondered, How could you feel even the most remote affection for a war criminal?

In maybe the same conversation, I expressed to Errol my dismay over the run-up to the wars in Afghanistan and Iraq, and I told him that I considered men like Donald Rumsfeld, Dick Cheney, and Paul Wolfowitz to be evil. I felt hatred for these men—the last of whom had a career very similar to my father's, because it also included a tenure at the World Bank. When I explained my feelings, Errol replied, "We tend to focus on one part of people, the part we can identify with. But people don't have to be one thing."

Errol doesn't believe in evil people; he believes in evil acts.

I suppose that this is a balanced point of view, but it isn't easy for me to accept it. It doesn't feel good to know that within my own family, close to my own heart and soul, there is capability for evil. I've tried to reconcile my affection and admiration for Dad—feelings Errol and I share—with the disturbing fact that, as the subject of an Errol Morris documentary, he's in a group with Donald Rumsfeld and Steve Bannon.

It would be easier to just be angry at him.

The Fog of War went on to win the Academy Award for Best Documentary in 2004. I have watched the film more than a dozen times since then. Every time, I look for something new and learn a little bit more about my father. I grieve for him. I see him in his final years, years in which he failed to take an interest in our lives, our family, the farm, and his grandchildren. In those last healthy years, every day not spent atoning for the past was a day spent etching his absence in our memories like runes in stone. I wish I had told Dad my thoughts on the film. I would have said to him, "I understand you. I forgive you. You had difficult decisions to make. You did your best. But you still did not tell the truth."

I suppose someone could watch the film and feel that the extreme close-ups are just a technical innovation. For me, the images are painfully revelatory. My father's face is aged, dehydrated, and spotted, yet still unmistakably the face of the confident young Defense chief with the slicked-back hair and severe gaze. I can't think of many times when my father looked me in the eye and spoke openly. Certainly not about his failures, certainly not for two hours.

There's one moment in the movie when Errol, from behind the interrotron, tries to ask Dad about how Vietnam affected his family. In the movie, Dad refuses to go there. He makes it clear that he wanted to shield his family from the painful parts of his career.

Trying to shield people doesn't work. A shield casts the shadow.

16.

His Final Days

Julie and I brought our three kids to Washington, DC, in April of 1992. Dad was at a Dutch Shell Oil board meeting in Europe and due to join us toward the end of our stay.

We did everything tourists do in DC, from cherry blossom walks to monument tours. I carried my daughter, Emily, just under a year and a half, in my backpack. We celebrated Easter around the same dining room table where three decades earlier, as a young boy, I sat patiently at breakfast while dad unfurled the Sunday *New York Times* and devoured every article.

Dad returned from his board meeting and joined us for our final days at 2412 Tracy Place. He held his granddaughter gingerly, with an inquisitive expression. It had been a long time since he had last held a toddler.

More than family life, his social life consumed him in these years. Before remarrying, he had a few intense romantic relationships. To the best of my knowledge, his affairs began in the mid-1980s, just a few years after Mom's death, and he continued to have different romances until he met his second wife. At times, I learned about his social life from news articles. For the most part, we didn't talk about it.

One of Dad's girlfriends was the beer manufacturing heiress Phyllis Coors. Several years ago, Phyllis's son emailed me a collection of letters written by Dad to Phyllis. They contain the most florid declarations of love. He shared poetry with her, reminisced about seeing *Titanic* with her, and even drew a lot of smiley faces. In certain correspondence, he apologizes for his "behavior," because he evidently pressured her to give up other relationships for him, and this evidently angered her. Along with the apologies come various promises to reform himself. In different cards, he refers to her as "the fairest of the fair" and even "one of God's loveliest creatures," which had also been his description of my mother. In March of 2000, Dad wrote to Phyllis, "My doctors say I will probably live an additional ten years. That means I would see you for a total of 240 hours during the remainder of my life…"

In that letter, Dad was trying to convince Phyllis to have lunch with him. He plays the role of the pursuer, almost begging, striving to spend every moment with a woman whom I must assume was embarrassed by him at times, and at other times flattered by his attention. There is desperation in these letters of a kind I never witnessed in him firsthand. It seems to me a tender, sweet, and unbearably sad state.

I don't think my father was equipped to live with that level of raw emotion. Leading up to his death, his emotional shields of power and prestige were truly compromised. I knew he was on antidepressants. I recall that there was talk of suicide. I can't remember now if I heard about this from his friends, one of my sisters, or the doctor who was treating him.

In the years between our time together in Telluride and

his death, we spoke regularly on the phone. By now Julie and I owned the farm outright, having purchased his shares from him, so the calls were less about business. We also wrote letters. My letters to him were warm, extremely loving, and communicative, but I often felt that he would reply only to specific requests. So I wrote to him to ask for donations to our agriculture education nonprofit and to arrange visits.

Birthdays were opportunities to remember the love between us. I planned a significant outing for his eightieth. We hired the same mountaineering outfit that we'd used when I was a child for a pack trip through the Sierras. At that age, Dad was still strong enough to hike.

Prior to the trip, Dad and Ben Eiseman, his best friend, were driving to Aspen in Ben's top-heavy truck. En route, they went off the road and flipped. Somehow they survived this accident and showed up for the start of the hike. Dad hardly talked about it, except to mention that he'd almost been scalped by a piece of the car door that had bent inward.

We hiked over the Sierras. He kept a good pace, and I rubbed his back by the campfire, like my mother had done when she was alive. Mules carried his gear. The younger members of the party carried their own gear. On the west side of the mountains, we arrived at the Ahwahnee Hotel for his birthday party.

By that time he was living in the Watergate in an apartment with a bedroom, kitchen, and living room, plus a storage unit in the basement filled with memorabilia, family keepsakes, and dozens of honorary degrees. I remember moving all these treasures out of the Tracy Place house. We spent days filling a dumpster, my sisters and children and I clandestinely saving various artifacts, because Dad wanted to throw almost everything away.

I often went to visit him in Washington. My son Sean was studying at Georgetown University, and he joined me for these visits. By that time Dad had remarried, and it was never comfortable for us to visit him and his second wife. There was a distance between us in those vulnerable years.

I tried so hard to bridge the divide. In his very last years, it was no longer about having a conversation about Vietnam, although I desperately wanted to. Now I just wanted my father back. I wanted him to be more involved in the lives of his grandchildren.

Things reached their nadir in 2006, when Dad broke his neck. It happened while he was walking to his office, just off the National Mall, and he tripped on a curb, a consequence of blustering and blundering through the city. His doctors gave him the option of wearing a metal contraption that would hold his head and neck in position until the fracture healed, which might take months, or undergoing an operation to fuse his head and neck together. He chose the operation.

The operation on his neck was a success. After almost sixty days in a rehab facility, Dad returned to the Watergate for bed rest. His recovery was not successful. His life, as I perceived it from the outside, started to deteriorate. The years ahead were tumultuous for him physically, and they were also tumultuous for our relationship. My journals from that time are filled with pages in which I record many attempts to fuse our lives. I remember sitting by his bed during one visit.

"Dad," I asked, "are you comfortable?"

"Yes."

"Are you happy?"

"Very happy."

"Is there anything that you need? Is there anything I can do to make your life more relaxed?"

"Oh, no. Thanks, Craigie."

Pause.

"Would you tell me if you weren't comfortable and happy?"

"No."

As his days blended with his nights, with him sleeping eighteen hours straight, Dad was not prepared to die. His mind wasn't sharp anymore. He talked about changes to his will. As his final months and days were approaching, Ben Eiseman said to him, "Bob, you're leaving a hell of a mess."

On my final visit to the Watergate, I held his frail hand in my freckled hand as he lay in what would be his deathbed. He said again and again that God had abandoned him.

"No, Dad," I replied. "Let go of that. God is blessing you."

"I'm abandoned."

I said "No, Dad. God has not abandoned you. Dad, he is holding you in the palm of his hand. He is asking you to let go. He wants to welcome you to Heaven. He is ready for you."

I'm not sure if Dad believed in Heaven. I do not, yet my words were sincere, because I do believe in a higher power. My father and I celebrated that higher power together throughout our lives: by drinking from mountain streams, feeling the wet kiss of dew as we awoke in our sleeping bags, and gliding through fluffy crystals of fresh snow on cross-country skis. To me, God is in nature, and nature abandons no one.

It's difficult, however, to find atonement in the silence of nature. There's no priest to confess to in the mountains. On Dad's ninetieth birthday, we had returned to the Ahwahnee, but by then he was using a wheelchair and unable to do the trek. My sister Margy had prepared a book and a speech to honor Dad's life and career. I wish that he had been able to make a speech himself in order to confess his misgivings, errors in judgment, honest mistakes, and arrogance; or to express his love for his family.

My father took the death of fifty-eight thousand US servicemen and servicewomen and millions of Vietnamese men, women, and children to his last hour. He died at 5:30 a.m. on July 6, 2009. I arrived at 6:30 after spending the night at Margy's house. It was Monday morning, and the sun hadn't yet entered the Watergate apartment. My father was lying in the dark dining room, which had been made up into a bedroom. The tightly drawn, freckled skin of his face and hands reminded me of the many times when sun and snow, strong mountain winds, and salty Atlantic water had touched those hands and face. I wondered if he was at peace.

I sat with the four-inch-thick DC Yellow Pages on my lap. My sister Kathleen had done some research and suggested that, when the time came, we call Gawler's funeral home in DC to arrange for Dad's cremation.

I started looking up the number for Gawler's. Leafing through the *G*s, getting closer to the *Ga*s, my finger was now on a left-hand page of the thick book. A thin ray of sunlight illuminated the carpet at my feet, but the book and my hands remained in darkness. As my gaze followed my finger down the thin pages of the phone book, I placed it on Gawler's. I called the number. A woman's voice answered the phone.

"My father has died, and I wondered if you could arrange for his cremation," I said.

She began to take down the information of his death and

the address of his Watergate apartment. A short time later, a woman in her fifties arrived. Her demeanor was kind and gentle. She quietly filled out the forms documenting my father's passing. Much later, a very senior man, possibly in his eighties, arrived, pushing a gurney. I remember thinking that he must be the woman's grandfather.

The gurney was draped in a scarlet coverlet that looked like it was from a bygone era. The old man was too frail to lift my father onto the gurney, so I gently lifted Dad up, holding him like a long babe in my arms. His body was stiff and slightly twisted, his mouth frozen open from his last breath. I could see the gold fillings in his teeth. I placed him on the antique gurney, covered him with the velvet blanket, and wheeled him out, first past Libby and Bob Dole's apartment, then past the doorman, and then into the alley, where a 1970s-style hearse awaited. We placed him in the hearse. Like that, I said goodbye to the man whom I had known and loved for fifty-nine years. To the woman and the old man, I said something to the effect of "You'll take good care of my father, won't you?"

As I reentered the apartment, the morning light was now coming in. I began to review the death certificate that had been filled out by the funeral home, and I realized that Gawler's hadn't completed it. I went back to the DC Yellow Pages and again thumbed through many inches of print. I realized that I had made a mistake. In the faint light, exhausted and dazed, I had inadvertently put my finger on the funeral home just under Gawler's, called Genesis. The ad read "Dignified and affordable direct cremation."

In somewhat of a panic, I called the woman from Genesis to confirm my mistake. She answered and said, "Oh, no,

Gawler's is much more expensive than we are. We are Genesis Funeral Home, and we saved you seven thousand dollars!"

Dad, forever the Scottish thrift, would have loved this surprise.

Together on Martha's Vineyard

My father always told me that he wanted to be buried with my mother in the Rocky Mountains and at Martha's Vineyard. He didn't want a funeral. He wanted to be remembered as a statesman who helped feed the poor and move the world toward peace. My family could never fulfill that last wish—nothing will ever dissociate his name from the Vietnam War—but we tried to give him a final rest that reflected the best parts of his life.

In September of 2009 our extended family came together on Martha's Vineyard to bury Dad's ashes with Mom's. My sisters,

Margy and Kathleen, came with their families. My cousin Rob, the son of my dad's sister Peg McNamara, came with his family. We carried pots of my mom's favorite flowers, peonies, to plant beside their grave. Julie had ordered a beautiful urn. We placed the remaining ashes inside and shared a program of photos and poems that we all took turns reading. Included in these were verses from George Santayana and T. S. Eliot and my parents' favorite Elizabeth Barrett Browning poem, "Sonnets from the Portuguese," which ends with these lines:

> *I love thee with a love I seemed to lose*
> *With my lost saints—I love thee with the breath,*
> *Smiles, tears, of all my life!—and, if God choose,*
> *I shall but love thee better after death.*

At the ceremony uniting my parents' ashes on a bluff overlooking South Beach, Martha's Vineyard

We buried their remains on an oak-and-pine-studded knoll overlooking Oyster Pond. It's a peaceful grove where two forgotten slate tombstones mark the passing of John and Mary on July 17, 1814, and July 29, 1814, respectively. Mary's age, as engraved on her tombstone, was ninety-two years and nine months. Mom and Dad would be honored to know that their neighbors in death lived long lives on the Vineyard.

A year or so later, a friend of ours was visiting President Kennedy's gravesite at Arlington Cemetery. As he was walking from the Kennedy graves up the hill to the Tomb of the Unknown Soldier, he spotted a large pink gravestone standing out from the thousands of gray granite tombstones. On it was inscribed:

Robert Strange McNamara
1916–2009
Secretary of Defense
1961–1968
Margaret Craig
1915–1981
Diana Masieri
1934

I never thought Dad wanted to be buried at Arlington. I am sure that walking by the graves of Vietnam War soldiers—if he ever did—brought him tremendous sadness during his final years in DC. Though we never discussed it, I imagine his second wife must have arranged the plot there, having saved some of his ashes.

When I think about this now, I feel the weight of a price that has been continually paid in ongoing tragedy. In the fields of the dead, Robert McNamara is linked with the true human cost of decisions he later wished not to have made.

Dad's tombstone at Arlington National Cemetery

I recall a time when Dad's determination overpowered me.

I was about fifteen years old, and we were skiing in the Swiss Alps. Together with a guide, we traversed a steep snowfield, attempting to climb up the mountain for a longer run down the glacier. The dense fog and snow slowly enveloped us until we were in a complete whiteout, with a thousand-foot fall below us and no idea which way was up or down. In extreme situations, a whiteout can make you dizzy, faint, and nauseated—exactly what I was feeling. I said to Dad that I thought it was time to turn around and that I would like to head back. He said, in no uncertain terms, "I'm not going back, and neither are you."

That "can and will" attitude and risky behavior are too deeply embedded to be forgotten. My son Sean and I were camping in the Colorado Rockies the summer after Dad's death. Our goal was to hike up to our favorite campsite, where Dad and I had buried my mom's ashes and where we later interred part of Dad's remains. It was June, and the winter snows had not yet begun to melt. We found one patch of snowless meadow to pitch our tent. We caught a beautiful rainbow trout in Snowmass Lake for dinner. The next day, we set off to find the trail to Mom's burial spot. Three feet of snow obscured the trail. I was sure we could find the pine tree that marked it, sure I could find the brass canister with the dates of Mom's life: August 22, 1915–February 3, 1981.

As we zigzagged through the woods, I had a sense of being lost, but my tenacity kept me going. Finally Sean said, "Dad, it's time to turn around."

All I wanted was to find Mom. I wasn't thinking about the fact that she lay beneath three feet of snow. But my son was. He understood that sometimes you shouldn't stay the course. I accepted what he said. In that moment, we communicated in a way that Dad and I never did. We turned around.

17.

The Chairs

Sometime after I lifted my father onto the gurney, probably the next day, my two sisters arrived at his apartment. We went over his will, which allowed Dad's wife to acquire all of his possessions and personal effects should she choose to do so. She did.

My sisters and I lost the Cuban Missile Crisis calendar; our parents' love letters and telegrams from World War II; Dad's Giacometti sculpture, Picasso paintings, and other art; scores of original letters; and many signed books from presidents, prime ministers, authors, and cartoonists.

One of the hardest things to lose was his desk, which was a gift from Kay Graham. The desk had belonged to Kay's father, Eugene Meyer, when he was chairman of the Federal Reserve and first president of the World Bank. Dad often told me that he hoped I would enjoy it upon his death.

My father's most memorable possessions, even more precious than the desk, were his cabinet chairs. They came into our family from Jackie Kennedy, just eight days after President Kennedy's assassination. There were two: one had been occupied by the President himself, the other by the loyal Defense czar. They were Chippendale armchairs: black leather upholstery, mahogany wood, silver nailhead trim. The brass plaque on the back of my father's chair was inscribed:

The Secretary of Defense | Robert S. McNamara |
Who from this Chair Served So Well | The President of the
United States | John Fitzgerald Kennedy |
Jan. 21, 1961–Nov. 22, 1963

My father's and JFK's cabinet chairs

I can't count how many times I sat in those chairs in our living room. Anytime I did, I experienced the same sensation: hope—New Frontier dreams. In my adult years, thinking I would receive the chairs upon Dad's death, they had come to represent a kernel of goodness. They embodied memories to keep and to hold. Maybe this is because the chairs were empty. They were not images of the men themselves. They awaited occupants and therefore could still represent hope. Ghosts could sit in them, and they could also seat the phantom of an alternate history.

We know how the story really turned out. In their cabinet chairs, the President and the secretary of defense sat together and agonized over the Bay of Pigs fiasco, the attempt to overthrow Castro. They tried to destroy a man whom I later came to greatly admire. Moreover, by early 1963, the Vietnam War was already escalating, and the two men seated in those beautiful chairs had already sent more than sixteen thousand US soldiers. There had already been over a hundred combat deaths. Perhaps, sitting in the chairs, they discussed the self-immolation of the Buddhist monk Thich Quang Duc at a busy Saigon intersection. President Kennedy said of a photograph of Duc on fire, "No news picture in history has generated so much emotion around the world as that one." Did he lean back as he said this, pressing his weight into the leather? Did he rest his elbows on the mahogany arms and hold the photograph over his lap, two sets of fingers grasping for a solution?

I wonder what memories the chairs stirred in Dad in his final months and days. I have to believe they were comforting to him. They represented the journey, the exploration, personified in one of his favorite poems by T. S. Eliot:

We shall cease from exploration
And the end of all our exploring
Will be to arrive where we started
And know the place for the first time

I remember a last vision of the chairs: a ray of dawn's light reflecting on the dark wood as my father lay dead in the adjoining dining room.

On October 23, 2012, the two cabinet chairs, along with over six hundred other pieces of personal memorabilia, were sold at a Sotheby's auction, timed to the fiftieth anniversary of the Cuban Missile Crisis. I have always assumed that my father's wife arranged to sell his possessions, though we never discussed it.

Prior to the actual auction, Sotheby's exhibited a collection called The White House Years of Robert S. McNamara. The exhibit went on for thirteen days, the same duration as the crisis. This was meant to build anticipation for the sale. The notes from the auction catalog read:

> In his memoir, Ted Sorensen, Special Counsel to President Kennedy, recalled that JFK considered McNamara to be the "star of his team, calling upon him for advice on a wide range of issues beyond national security, including business and economic matters." Sotheby's sale of The White House Years of Robert S. McNamara features private papers and memorabilia from his tenure as Secretary of Defense, including his appointment from President Kennedy, extensive correspondence from Mrs. Kennedy, gifts from world leaders, and furnishings from his office and the Cabinet Room.

The auction lots were an eclectic mix—from my father's California boyhood to the years of the Camelot White House and the tumult of the Vietnam War. The sale included handwritten letters; autographed photos of JFK, RFK, and LBJ;

a cache of medals; Dad's Eagle Scout badge from 1933; his colorful Presidential Medal of Freedom; his official secretary of defense flag from the Pentagon; presidential signing pens and inaugural tokens; North Vietnamese propaganda; notes on *The Fog of War*; and volumes of political cartoons about him, warmly inscribed by the individual artists.

When I first got my hands on the Sotheby's catalog, I didn't entirely believe what I was reading. This was the dream version of our lives, in which we went to Washington, DC, and Dad became secretary of defense, and we all became a part of history. Turning those pages, I felt for a moment that I was about to wake up in my bed, a young boy in Ann Arbor, Michigan, the son of a prominent auto executive, and proceed with my proper lifetime.

The auction was in New York. With obligations on the farm, I couldn't attend in person. So I called Sotheby's to request a representative.

My wife, Julie, and sister Margy lovingly offered to purchase Dad's calendar from the Cuban Missile Crisis. They had settled on this memento because they knew it meant a lot to me. I had attempted to purchase it in advance of the auction; this request was denied. Ultimately my sister, my wife, and I agreed on a ceiling price.

When the day arrived, I wasn't optimistic. The catalog listed the calendar as lot number 20, with bidding beginning at $15,000 to $25,000. That was already way beyond my financial comfort zone.

Julie and I sat together in the farm office. The auction began at 10 a.m. East Coast time. I'm told by the person who was there that the calendar was prominently displayed.

Within minutes of the opening gavel, the chairs were sold for $146,500. My heart was broken, even though I knew this was coming. For so long, it had been my selfish dream to share the cabinet chairs with my two sisters.

Soon they announced bidding for the calendar. The auctioneer's voice was loud and clear through our phone connection.

"Do I hear fifteen—fifteen thousand dollars?"

My heart sank. Within seconds, the price approached our ceiling. It truly felt as if time were speeding up. There was so much tension in the office where Julie and I sat.

They asked for an increased bid, $5,000 more. Our bidder asked, "Yes or no?" I said yes. Just like that, we blew by our cap. The auctioneer's voice was steady, almost sweet, as the price kept ascending.

"Do I hear eighty thousand?"

I said, "No." Too high.

But I countered. I asked my bidder if the auctioneer would accept $77,500. She doubted it.

"Will you take a bid of seventy-seven five?"

"Final bid?"

At last, I heard the words, "Sold—at seventy-seven thousand five hundred dollars!"

I let out a breath, long held in. There was no sense of celebration, no victory. Something that had been important in my life was returning, and I would be the steward of it, but it never should have been lost in the first place. I was fortunate that we had the collective means for this, but we shouldn't have had to bid on my memories. The auction left me feeling abandoned by him, even in his death.

I also felt that I had asked too much of Julie and my sister.

In the office, Julie and I stood up. We hugged each other, and I thanked her. It was her earnings and Margy's earnings that made this possible.

About a month after the auction, a FedEx truck backed up to the farm and delivered a handcrafted three-by-four-foot box. In it was the three-by-four-inch Cuban Missile Crisis calendar, wrapped in multiple layers of protective material. With the commission to Sotheby's, the shipping, and the insurance, the final bill for the calendar was over $100,000. That was the price for reaching far into the past and reclaiming a memory of my father: sitting across from him, hugging him, kissing his cheek, smelling the scotch he was drinking while he ran his fingers over that small silver tile.

18.

Vietnam

My father went to Hanoi in 1995. In the press the trip was described as his return to Vietnam. He had just published his memoir, *In Retrospect*. During his visit to Hanoi, he would meet with General Vo Nguyen Giap, the leader of the North Vietnamese military and his onetime nemesis.

I very much wanted to join Dad on this trip. Selfishly, I wanted to go on a journey of discovery, to experience a place that had indirectly defined so much of my life. As my father's son, I wanted to be there as he sought closure and attempted to heal the open wounds he helped create. As an American citizen, I wanted to learn and educate myself about Vietnamese perspectives on the American War.

The trip would be in autumn, and the harvest was approaching, our busiest time, and walnut prices were down. We were losing money on about 120 acres of land that I had painstakingly planted fifteen years prior. It was land I dearly loved, but I would end up having to sell it to my neighbors to stay in the black.

Anticipating the start of harvest at the end of our work-days, worrying about the health of the soil and the instability of our production, I felt defeated. This failing acreage was a problem I couldn't solve. Despite that, in the autumn of 1995, I was willing to put aside farming for a moment. For the chance to accompany my father to Vietnam, I would have left my post.

I called him up from my farm office. He was probably in his office at Corning Glass, where he sat at Kay Graham's old desk. It began like our other conversations. "How's the walnut crop looking?" I explained to Dad that it was going to be a tough year for us. I felt my throat tightening. Getting ready to make a request. At that time, asking people for things was very difficult for me.

Finally I gathered a breath and asked him about the Vietnam trip. I made it clear that I wanted to come. Then I asked, "Is Nick's grandson really going?"

I had heard this from John Katzenbach, my lifelong friend. Dad confirmed it. Nick Katzenbach was part of the retinue going to Hanoi, and his grandson was included. But I was excluded.

I told Dad that I really wanted to go.

"Oh, I don't really think it would be appropriate," he replied.

In 1995, Nick's grandson's presence felt like a usurpation. I had nothing against him, but I felt strongly that I too needed to be involved. Looking back, I think what I felt was the desire to be with my father. I wanted to be there for him and with him. I wanted to say, "Just be with me, Dad."

As we spoke on the phone, the physical distance between

us grew tangible. After that he got quiet. We hung up. It was like a great exhale. I didn't cry.

When he went to Hanoi, I went back to the harvest. I tried to recalibrate my energies around work. I turned to the land, over which the light of the season was changing and the temperature was dropping, creating a chill of nervous anticipation. To distract myself from the pain of rejection and the uncertainties of walnut prices, I put my energies into making the operation efficient. Every morning, I met with our farm team at 6:30. From there the day unfolded with pure momentum. I received the walnut truck coming in and pulling alongside our warehouse, and I directed the driver to park underneath the load-out conveyor belt. It was still dark in the early morning, so I turned the side light on and offered the truck driver a cup of coffee. As the day proceeded, I ran between various parts of the harvest, troubleshooting.

Two decades passed before I thought about traveling to Vietnam on my own.

Why didn't I take the initiative sooner? Certainly I had traveled enough: to Mexico and to Chile, to Colorado for family vacations, to DC for visits with my father. There is no single reason why I didn't go sooner. Among the many reasons were the pain of the war and the impossibility—for me as a noncombatant—of fully confronting its far-reaching consequences.

Maybe it was simply too difficult while Dad was still alive.

There was a turning point in January of 2012, when I was contacted for the first time by Sarah Botstein, who was producing a documentary on the Vietnam War with Ken Burns and Lynn Novick. A few months later, the documentary team arranged a trip to Winters to interview me. I went to therapy in preparation because I felt vulnerable and torn about what to say and what not to say. The interview might be a chance to distance myself from my father. My therapist reminded me, "It's still important to protect yourself in this process." Till then I hadn't thought about it in that way. It seemed like my father's story, not mine.

The camera crew set up their equipment in the hallway that leads from my bathroom to the kitchen. I sat between our kitchen and living room. The interview ended up lasting a few hours. When it was over, I immediately wondered if I had been honest enough, if I had said enough. The interview felt like the pendulum of my whole life—swinging between feelings that were radically charged and plain affection for Dad.

I watched every episode of the eighteen-hour documentary. As I viewed it, I became self-conscious about how I would come across in my interview segment. I also wondered how hard the documentary was going to be on my father.

Probably one of the most striking moments was a clip of my father in Vietnam, speaking before a crowd and grasping the hand of Prime Minister Nguyen Khanh. Dad, facing the microphone, tried to speak Vietnamese. He intended to say, "Vietnam ten thousand years," a phrase used to wish long life—or in this case, "Long live Vietnam." However, his pronunciation was off, and to Vietnamese listeners it sounded like he said, "Ruptured duck wants to lie down." To me, this clip showed that Dad tried awkwardly to empathize with people he didn't really understand. He tried to speak the language, tried to deliver a message of unity, and he completely bungled it.

Besides the parts about my father, the film changed my understanding of the war's long history. Before I saw it, I had little knowledge of the history of the French occupation. Diem Bien Phu, General Giap, President Diem—these were names to me at most. Even my involvement in the peace movement as a young man had left gaps in what I understood. I didn't know the extent to which Martin Luther King opposed the war, and I had only a vague sense of the many connections between Vietnam and the civil rights movement.

I had wanted so desperately to learn about Vietnam from my father. Even in the last years of his life, when I prioritized his health and comfort, I think part of me never gave up on the idea of having that conversation—the one in which he would fully explain to me his role in history, and his own point of view.

I felt the grief of those lost opportunities, and I sought other conversations instead of the one I should have had with my father. After Dad's death, I was lucky to befriend Daniel Ellsberg, the whistleblower and historian who leaked the Pentagon Papers. Through conversations with Dan at his home in Berkeley, I learned things about my father's career that I couldn't have processed on my own, even if I had read them in a book.

Dan has given me the gift of conversations I once thought I would have with my father. Still, learning history from a primary source hasn't made up for the emotional unburdening I needed from Dad. I am not a historian or an intellectual; I'm a farmer. In my life I've gone away from my father's way of understanding the world and his interpretation of history. I crave to experience things and see things at the ground level.

I came very close to traveling to Vietnam with Rich Rusk, the son of Dean Rusk, who was the secretary of state and my father's colleague during the Kennedy and Johnson administrations. Rich was another person with whom I wanted to discuss history—our personal histories and our fathers' roles.

I met Rich over email in 2015. It was an unexpected message. Rich told me that he had interviewed Dad for a book he wrote with his own father, *As I Saw It*.

"For whatever it is worth," Rich wrote to me, "I loved your father. Another good man who did his very best."

We exchanged many emails, in which I learned Rich's life story. In 1970, having become estranged from his father over Vietnam, Rich moved to Alaska and took up fishing. His was a story not unlike mine—except that Rich didn't speak with his father for fourteen years.

It amazed me that I had never met Rich in person. We shared a common experience that few people have. In one email, he wrote to me about attending his father's swearing-in as secretary of state. We must have been in the East Room of the White House together. My father stood next to Dean Rusk at that event.

In 2017, Rich was preparing to travel to Vietnam with a tour group that included veterans. In one of his last emails to me, he shared a letter he had written to the organizers of the tour. He wanted me to edit it for him because he was anxious about how he would come across to a community of veterans.

Craig, any thoughts on a Rusk touring Vietnam with antiwar activists? My son Andy will be going with me.

Given the antiwar composition, agenda and mission of this tour, I thought it best to ask tour organizers.

Is it appropriate?

Still wish you were going!

---------- Forwarded message ----------

It was Dean Rusk, the former secretary of state who, along with JFK, LBJ, and Robert McNamara, were primarily responsible for American policy during 1968, the worst year of the war, and the events—Tet Offensive, Khe Sanh, My Lai—we will be commemorating.

Question: would my presence on this tour have any negative or inhibiting influence on our band of brothers? I would hope not...but still need to ask.

We share a common bond in opposing the war. This includes the architects of 1968. I adored the man as his son, but many of us probably disliked—and some even hated—Dean Rusk, Robert McNamara and the others. They have reasons for doing so....

We have all earned the right to our views, especially the veterans among us. As a tour participant, I will be quieter than most, bearing witness to it all. If ever called upon to speak, it will be from the heart with words of gratitude, respect and admiration to all who opposed the Vietnam War and did their best to end it. Thanks to Chuck and Veterans for Peace, now we are doing our best to heal from it.

Rich Rusk

Chuck Searcy, the organizer of the trip, was Rich's life-long friend. He had served in Vietnam and joined Vietnam Veterans Against the War after returning home. His life has been dedicated to healing wounds and working toward peace. He had organized this trip for Vietnam veterans, their spouses, and peace activists. It was timed to coincide with the fiftieth anniversary of the My Lai massacre. My Lai, in many ways, epitomized the evil of the American War: the misguided objectives; the horror of the atrocities committed against Vietnamese civilians; the tragedy of the young Americans committing those atrocities, destroying a peaceful village and slaughtering unarmed families, fathers, mothers, and children. The soldiers' conduct would come to be seen through the structural lens of military policy, especially the body-count principle—the idea forwarded by war planners that we would win in Vietnam by killing more of their people than they killed of ours. Body counts, of course, were among the statistics demanded by the Defense Department.

The trip was a unique opportunity for Rich. After writing a book with his father, it must have been deeply moving for him to think about traveling on a mission of peace with his own son. I spoke to him by phone several times in the weeks leading up to his trip. I was touched that he wanted me to come with him, and I was excited by the idea of one day meeting him in person.

Our phone conversations were the closest contact we ever had. On January 28, 2018, just weeks before he was scheduled to travel to Vietnam, Rich committed suicide by jumping off a bridge. When I heard the news, I thought about the enormity of the loss for his son and the rest of his family.

Chuck Searcy wrote to me afterward, saying, "Rich had

tried for so many years to figure out a schedule and finances to allow him to come to Viet Nam. He told me many times, 'I really need to do that. I've got to do it—for me and my dad.'"

It's not possible for me to know why Rich killed himself. I only know that he was one of the few people on earth with experiences comparable to mine. Sons of controversial historical figures, we were linked by that war even though we didn't participate as soldiers. Not meeting Rich in person is something I profoundly regret.

I didn't think of it this way at the time, but it's possible that my conversations with Rich finally pushed me to prioritize traveling to Vietnam. I discussed a trip around the dinner table in the farmhouse, and Julie supported the idea. When the dates were set, my daughter, Emily, was able to take some time off work to accompany me.

In preparation for our trip I read Philip Caputo's devastating account *A Rumor of War* and Tim O'Brien's heartbreaking book *The Things They Carried*. I also read Nguyen Qui Duc's eloquent tale *Where the Ashes Are*, a book recommended to me by my friend Nhu Miller. Compared with my awareness of the many books written by American historians or veterans, I had very little knowledge of the landscape of accounts by Vietnamese writers.

I spent time meeting and speaking with friends in California who had served in Vietnam. I relied very much on the help of Nhu and her husband, Tom Miller. Over the phone and at their home in Berkeley, the Millers connected me with relatives in Vietnam who could be my hosts. Nhu introduced me to her Vietnamese in-law Le Nuoi, who lives in Hoi An, a city on the central coast of the country.

I felt I needed a guide in Hanoi, and for this, I relied on the help of my friend Bob Mulholland, who served in the war and whom I'd met through my leadership work in California agriculture. Bob connected me with Thao Griffiths. At the time we were planning our trip, Thao was helping to organize an international conference on economic development that Vietnam was hosting. She had also been there for my father's trip in 1995. As a diplomacy student, she had been called upon to serve as a "protocol girl," dressing up to welcome Robert S. McNamara, holding flowers as his entourage passed by on the way to meeting General Giap. Now Thao would be my guide and teacher on a trip I was making with my daughter.

I felt one of the infinite circles of life, containing myself and that far-off place, being closed.

When Emily and I arrived in Hanoi, Thao swept us up. On our first morning, she met me at 5 a.m. outside the Metropole Hotel, riding on a scooter. She wanted to show me the street culture, and I was happy to ride along. We went to the French Quarter and visited Ly Thai To park. In the park, hundreds of people were doing morning exercises, such as laughing yoga and tai chi. Kids were playing soccer. Couples were practicing ballroom dancing. As Thao and I strolled through the crowd, a middle-aged woman grabbed me and started dancing with me for a minute. I had no thought of withdrawing or shrinking back.

Beyond the park, the hum of Hanoi was everywhere. Street vendors laid their wares down on cloth coverings on the sidewalks and side streets. Thao and I ate varieties of street food, sitting on plastic stools and dipping our fingers into fish sauce. While we ate, I watched women from the countryside carry baskets of greens on their backs, and I pondered the difference between the agriculture I was witnessing and my farming experiences in the United States.

This all took place in the first few hours of my first morning in Vietnam. Watching the street economy, I understood Thao's predilection for getting up early. The day soon became overpoweringly hot and humid. Everything I saw in these early hours of our trip suggested a sense of life lived at a frantic pace, of life crowding around me, an unknown traveler. Walking the streets was a strong contrast to the black-and-white images of Hanoi from the Burns-Novick documentary and newspaper photographs of war-torn countryside.

Of course, nobody on the street knew my identity. I had the feeling of being embraced, but maybe that was only because of my anonymity. How many people in the park had relatives on either side of the war? I don't want to see every person in Vietnam as a victim; yet there persists a sadness about the remote possibility that I danced in the street with someone who had lost a family member to bombs dropped by Robert McNamara.

Hurrying to keep up with Thao, I thought about the trip I didn't make with Dad. Of his time in Hanoi, I've heard that he appeared haunted, and that his presence was haunting. People stared, but he didn't look back. This is only what I've been told. Walking the streets and surrounded by an entourage, he wasn't open to people. I think about him heading to his office in Washington in his old age, how he warded cars off with a newspaper, barreling through the streets without regard for other people, yelling at motorists and grumbling to himself. Maybe he knew more about the war than I did, but Dad didn't allow himself the joy of being in Vietnam as I did.

*   *   *

One day, Thao was leading Emily and me through a crowded area along the bank of the Red River, full of motorcycle and bicycle traffic. Thao stopped us and said, "I really want you to meet a friend of mine."

She didn't say who it was, but I could tell that it meant a lot to her, so Emily and I agreed to go along. In seconds, Thao waved down two motorcycles and persuaded their drivers to take us to her friend's house. We jumped on the backs of the bikes and rode on a train trestle in the wrong direction, going against traffic, skirting the edge of the street. At a certain place above the river, the bikes jumped off the train tracks and went down a steep embankment through thistles and scrub. Thao led us along the shore to a small houseboat, constructed mostly out of driftwood, with a chicken coop outside made from the same material. She rang the doorbell, and the three of us entered the houseboat together.

The woman who lived there was formerly homeless and looked old. She served us tea and spoke in Vietnamese with Thao. She lived on the boat with her husband, Thao explained. Through some means, Thao and her friends had procured the boat and also arranged for the two of them to get married.

Thao didn't explain to us exactly what this friendship meant to her. Only that she wanted to share it. I thought it showed her love for the people of her country, a sense that even anonymous citizens on the streets and riverbanks mattered to her. After the short visit, thanking her for the tea, we left the woman's house. We walked back up the bank, got on the trestle, and returned to the busy street.

*   *   *

On the morning we met Vo Hong Nam, I awoke at 4 a.m. to rendezvous with Thao. The traffic was just beginning as we made our way to Hanoi's largest flower market. As we motored along the dike separating the Red River from the city, I could make out the most exquisite ceramic mural I have ever seen. Its rich color and design reflected the complexity and vibrancy of Hanoi. Thao told me that it was the world's largest ceramic mosaic, at four kilometers long.

Arriving at the flower market, we sidestepped through aisle after aisle of gorgeous tropical flowers. I picked out four dozen of the freshest long-stemmed roses. Each tiny rosebud was wrapped in tissue paper. At first I thought this was a waste of someone's labor; later I appreciated it as we sped through Hanoi on motor scooters, with the wind jostling forty-eight rosebuds held tightly in my arms.

When we arrived at the house, we were met by Nam and his wife, Rose. They asked us to join them in the garden. They had a peaceful patio behind one of the oldest residences in Hanoi, originally occupied by the French governor Henri Hoppenot. It was a stucco villa, faded yellow with green shutters. Ho Chi Minh had given this home to General Giap after he defeated the French at the battle of Diem Bien Phu.

Nam is the youngest son of General Giap. I am just a few years older than him. We are two sons of two fathers involved in the same struggle. His father came to be revered; mine came to be hated. He was in Vietnam for the American War. I was in America during the Vietnam War.

The garden was welcoming, with the general's koi pond at its center. Surrounding the pond, a tall trellis supported baskets of deep green ferns and climbing roses. Nam explained to me that the gray canisters supporting the trellis were casings from US bombs dropped on Hanoi. I didn't ask whether the bombs had struck close to the home where he now lived.

Together, the four of us—Nam, Rose, Thao, and I—squatted on our haunches on the patio tile, trimming rose stems and placing them in large brass urns. Our conversation was that of new acquaintances, curious about the past and present, filled with kindness and respect. Had the roles been reversed, with Nam and Rose arriving at our farm in California on a summer day, I could envision us greeting each other in the same way, peacefully accepting a gift.

I followed Nam and Rose up the steps into a room of their home that housed the shrine of his father. As we entered the shrine, we removed our shoes and lit incense, placing it on the altar adorned with fresh fruit. We placed our roses on the altar. Nam took my hand. Together, we bowed in silence. On the wall behind me was a large portrait of the general in uniform, a warm smile on his face, made from a collage of over three thousand smaller photos of him.

We then crossed the patio to the general's formal meeting room. The walls, bookshelves, and tables—every square inch—were covered with photos, statues, medals, banners, plaques, and memorabilia from the general's long life. In this room, Vo Nguyen Giap had met with hundreds of leaders from around the world. I saw statues of Uncle Ho and Chairman Mao, as well as photos of Fidel Castro, Leonid Brezhnev, Chilean president Michelle Bachelet, Brazilian president Lula da Silva, Jacques Chirac, and so many more.

As we sat and talked, Nam presented me with a recently

released book celebrating his father's life. As we leafed through the pages, I found on page 165 a photo of General Giap and my father taken on November 9, 1995. The caption read: "The most brilliant Vietnamese general was the Vietnamese people, the Vietnamese nation. The Americans were defeated by Viet Nam because they did not yet understand that general."

Those words caught my eye, and I said to Nam, "Both of our fathers were called to duty without a significant military background."

And yet my father was synonymous with the war in the minds of Americans. I mentioned this to Nam.

With my counterpart, Vo Hong Nam, the son of General Giap, at the general's home in Hanoi with his wife, Rose (standing), and Thao Griffiths

He replied, "I think that when my father met your father, he said, 'Americans didn't understand Vietnamese culture and history.' And he was so right."

As Nam and I sat together privately, somewhat formally but without presumption, I thought of the intimacy of our meeting. No cameras were there, other than Thao snapping some friendly photos. There were no articles written about our meeting. We met, we talked; we saw each other. Then we made our way back into life.

Emily and I traveled to many parts of the country after Hanoi. We traveled together, then separately, and we had many hosts and guides. In Hue, the second major city on our itinerary, Chuck Searcy was my shepherd. He was preparing to lead the My Lai commemoration trip that Rich Rusk was supposed to go on.

One afternoon, Chuck and I were driving on a road through a forested area, and he told me that we were going to pass something called the McNamara Line, an installation in the former DMZ where my father had conceived of dropping a series of electronic sensors from planes in order to pick up enemy troop movements. It didn't work, Chuck explained to me, because the cutting-edge sensors frequently picked up the sounds of animals and other ambient noise. Chuck said that there was a carved stone slab in the jungle somewhere commemorating this folly of Robert McNamara.

As we were driving, I spotted something off the road. "Wait," I said. "Is that it?"

Chuck hit the brakes. We got out of the car and went off the road, hacking through a few feet of jungle with a machete. There was a plaque not unlike the marker I had made for my mother's grave. It read, according to Chuck's translation:

The "Magic Eye" of the McNamara Electronic Fence, an evidence of the humiliating defeat of the U.S. Empire in 1975

In Hue, Chuck had done a lot of work to commemorate the victims of ordnance explosions, past and present. He took me to a museum that he had helped construct that contained several exhibits about the effects of Agent Orange. As I recall it, we had also planned some visits with families whose adult children were affected by chemical warfare, but the plan fell through. I wanted to feel that pain, to know what my father's actions continued to deliver.

Looking back on my trip, I realize that I saw little evidence of physical destruction in the landscape. In fact, I saw a country that had done much to heal. The beauty of Vietnam—its mountains and rivers and vast green spaces—stood in contrast to what I knew about the history of the war. This made me happy as a farmer and an environmentalist; it made me uncomfortable too, because I felt a responsibility to get closer to the pain and the suffering. On the other hand, I wondered if it was my place to do that. Maybe the magnitude of the suffering is too great for me to properly acknowledge.

In Hue we stayed in a colonial hotel. The architecture of that city is largely French. My North American mind reacted positively then, and still does, to colonial columns and baroque spirals—ornate things, the pretty artifacts of conquest. Later, in Saigon (now Ho Chi Minh City), Emily rejoined me. We arrived there during a downpour and visited a house that had belonged to Henry Cabot Lodge Jr., the US ambassador to

South Vietnam in the early years of US involvement. Our hosts there ran a large tour company. Stepping into the house, we stepped back into 1965. The homeowners had restored a part of the house as a kind of museum of the period. There were pictures of my father on the wall with General Maxwell Taylor. In our socks, we climbed to the second floor of the house and peered into the small guest room where my father slept during his many visits to Saigon.

I don't think I cried much on this trip, and I don't think I had many nightmares. Still, I felt my father's shadow. The plaque, the photos. He was there, I thought, in the eyes of people I met: a dragon-fruit farmer who had been a member of the Viet Cong; two young artists who made replica uniforms of North and South Vietnamese soldiers; and others I don't remember. In my limited time in the country, I felt the absence that defined our relationship. So much of being my father's son has been contained in that feeling of a missed connection and the inability to mark certain tragedies, so they linger.

19.

The Cathedral Block

I went back to Stanford in the winter of 2018. At age sixty-eight, I was returning to the campus where fifty years earlier I had spent most of my time protesting. Together with Julie, I took art, literature, and history classes. It was during this time that I finally read *In Retrospect* in its entirety. I think traveling to Vietnam had finally liberated me to begin a more complete investigation of my father's career—which is ongoing to this day.

For one of my classes, I attended a lecture by the Stanford art historian Alexander Nemerov. Sitting in the dim lecture hall, I listened as Nemerov analyzed a political cartoon by Emory Douglas, the Black Panther Party's revolutionary artist and minister of culture. The cartoon depicts dead pigs hung from a tree. The pigs represent some major figures from the Johnson administration: LBJ, RFK, Dean Rusk, and my father. The pig representing my dad is labeled "Mad McNamara."

To see my father lynched as a pig was horrifying. I still saw those pigs as good men who made bad decisions. Yet as I listened to the lecture and processed the cartoon on the projector screen, my main reaction was silent agreement. If Dad had seen it, how would he have reacted? I know that he wouldn't have smiled. He was not so dismissive of Americans' anger. He would feel anger toward himself, I'm sure, plus some indifference, sadness, and guilt. His critics never moved him to change his actions.

A cartoon by Emory Douglas shows the Black Panthers' view of my father, LBJ, RFK, and Dean Rusk. The caption reads: ON LANDSCAPE ART "It is good only when it shows the oppressor hanging from a tree by his motherf--king neck." -- EMORY. (© 2022 Emory Douglas / Artists Rights Society [ARS], New York)

In our small farming community of Winters, it's common for the old-timers to have nicknames. Just like when I was in boarding school, the nicknames reflect a cartoonish image, whether wholly imagined or somewhat accurate. There's "College Joe," who went to college. "Windy Martin" tends to be verbose. I'm not aware of all the nicknames I've garnered in town, but I'm aware of one.

During the later years of my farming career, having served on state and local agricultural boards, I gained some political detractors. One of these was a farmer from outside Winters who featured himself as the conservative backbone of the county, serving on the county board of supervisors and the county Farm Bureau. Any time this man spoke about me, he referred to me as "Communist." Whenever possible, he'd confront me with slurs or distribute pamphlets at Farm Bureau meetings that sought to demonstrate that I was not a farmer but a socialist.

The last time I saw him, I had been invited by the president of the Farm Bureau to provide a briefing on the state of agriculture in California. After I was introduced, before I got up to speak, my right-wing detractor bolted to the dais, clutching a stack of xeroxed papers (at least two feet high), which he distributed to the board members. These included news articles about my travels to the socialist country of Chile, rallies that I attended, and pro-democracy speeches that I'd given at Newman Catholic Center in Davis. My successful countywide opposition to a "New Town" of six thousand people, which would have converted a thousand acres of agricultural land into residential development, was also in there.

After handing out his literature, my local nemesis launched into a twenty-minute tirade about how I was a Communist, attempting to bring land reform to the county and—worst of all—higher wages to farmworkers.

I was caught completely off guard. I looked straight into the faces of the board members, half of whom I knew and had worked with closely over many years. Not one of them came to my defense. Nor did the president of the board gavel this tirade out of order. When the man finally sat down, I stood up, thanked the board for their invitation, and presented my update on the state of agriculture in California—pretending that nothing unusual had happened.

After the meeting, as I walked out into the night air, I wondered how Bob McNamara would have handled the situation. Dad once talked about nearly "coming to blows" with a detractor during a diplomatic trip, but that was not believable to me. In my experience, he always endured criticism with silence.

When I arrived home and stepped into our kitchen, Julie said, "You look a little pale." In almost the same moment, the phone rang. It was one of my farmer friends who served on the board, who had attended the meeting. He began to apologize for not having stood up for me, and then he let me know that the man who liked to call me Communist always packed a weapon, either on his person or in his truck.

My response to being berated at the board meeting was not unlike Dad's when he walked off the stage at Zellerbach Hall. I was being judged, pushed out of my comfort zone, and I didn't offer any rebuttal. At a minimum, I could have acknowledged what happened. Maybe it would have humanized me to my detractor, and vice versa. Politically, my situation was the opposite of what Dad confronted as the foil of left-wing protesters. But neither of us took responsibility for somehow reducing the distance. Doesn't this go against Dad's first lesson: "Empathize with your enemy"?

I had not thought very much about how isolating his fame and infamy must have been. That night, I went to sleep thinking of myself as my father's son.

Many years after my father died, my friend Mimi Haas revealed to me the fate of his cabinet chairs. In the winter of 2016, she had traveled to Mexico City for an exhibition organized by the San Francisco Museum of Modern Art. There she met Danh Vo, a visual artist who was born in Vietnam.

It was Danh who ultimately became the curator of the chairs. His representative, the world-renowned gallerist Marian Goodman, had purchased them at auction, intending to turn them over to Danh. Marian herself had been a Vietnam War protester in the 1960s.

Prior to contacting Danh Vo, I went to see his work on display in San Francisco. Entering the exhibition at SFMOMA, I recalled how I once thought of the cabinet chairs as valuable fixtures in my childhood home. Then I saw Danh's work. The piece was called *Two Kennedy Administration Cabinet Room Chairs*. Danh had dismantled the chairs, pulling out the horsehair-and-cotton stuffing. This material, once used to cushion seats of power, now lay on the gallery floor. The black leather upholstery hung from the wall with the muslin and burlap linings. Hanging there, the material of the chairs was weighed upon by gravity now rather than resisting it as an upright construction. The loose skin of the chairs recalled to me how the leather came from an animal, the skin of living things now dead. The only remaining element of the original chairs was their bare mahogany bones: a chair without a cushion, leather, or comfort. Danh had literally taken the chairs apart, and each part had become an artistic statement.

Danh used the chairs to tell a story about America and Vietnam, memory and imagination, the fixed nature of legacy and the open possibilities of the future. Within weeks, Danh and I were in touch.

Dear Craig,

I can't tell you how happy I was to receive your email. At the moment I'm traveling in the countryside of Vietnam, crossing into China. I just wanted to write you a short email to confirm that I got your message, but will get back to you in the beginning of the New Year, when my feet are grounded. For now, happy New Year.

Danh Vo

Danh's messages came to me from all over the world: Berlin, Mexico City, Vietnam, Joshua Tree, Kyoto. I thought the fact that he wrote so little was fascinating; clearly this was a person whose deeds and works spoke for him. Soon we were speaking on the phone.

Danh changed the way I thought about Vietnam and my father. There was suddenly a handhold in the darkness. When I stared up at that cream-colored wall on the seventh floor of SFMOMA, where Danh had created a tapestry from upholstery twine and cushion nails, I witnessed the war as somebody else might see it, with some objectivity. And I realized that the chairs never belonged to me. Where I had envisioned them as symbols of Camelot and courage, they could also be seen as thrones of violence. The dream I had harbored as a thirteen-year-old boy of someday adorning my living room with the chairs now seemed revealed as a mask for more complex truths, and for my own anger. In my house, the chairs would have been nothing more than objects of pain and desire. In the museum, they could belong to everyone who saw the exhibit. As art, they could belong to everyone in the world, even to collective memory and consciousness.

Marian Goodman explained to me that it had been Danh's idea to purchase the chairs.

"I felt really badly when the chairs were broken down," she said. "Because I felt they must mean a lot to the family."

I assured Marian of the opposite. For me, seeing Danh's work freed me from the burden of the chairs. Danh, in Marian's words, "made them perform," and this made their deconstruction worth it.

Danh Vo was born in Vietnam in 1975. In 1979, his family fled South Vietnam in a homemade boat as part of the enormous wave of refugees who left the country after the devastation wrought over years during the American War. They were rescued at sea by a Danish commercial vessel and consequently repatriated as Danish citizens. From these beginnings, Danh eventually rose to the Danish Royal Academy of Fine Arts and international success in the art world. His is the sort of rags-to-riches success story that is often used to illustrate the American Dream. In reality, American failures arguably set the stage for Danh's triumphs.

He first came to our farm in Winters in the spring of 2017. We spent two days deep in conversation, taking daytime walks through the orchards. He was an amazing, unique houseguest. Without a moment of hesitation, he might drop everything and start preparing a meal for us. If the mood struck him, he would suddenly start washing dishes. Both social and private, he would talk with me for hours, and he would just as comfortably withdraw to the walnut orchards to contemplate the land alone and have a smoke.

I remember many conversations in the farmhouse living room. We would cook dinner and eat around the fireplace and stay up late, drinking wine and cocktails—and, later, coffee to stay awake. I remember watching my oldest son, Graham, seated in a living room chair in the dim light of the fire, listening intently as Danh described how he was becoming more interested in incorporating land and soil into his artwork.

On that evening, I identified so strongly with Graham. This was the sort of thing that Bob McNamara and I never did. Welcoming Danh presented us with an opportunity to respond to Dad's war-making legacy. It might not change what Dad did, but it was better than decades of deflection and deliberate silence.

Years later, when Danh visited the farm again, I confessed how blessed I felt for his friendship.

"To think, if she hadn't done that..."

I meant my dad's wife, who sold the chairs. In retrospect, this statement also applies to Marian, who had felt some hesitation about buying them for Danh to dismember.

"It's a lucky star," Danh said. Coming to our farm and appreciating nature had unlocked a new interest, a new love of the earth.

"If you asked me three years ago about anything in nature," he told me, "I would have had no clue. And probably I would have looked at you and said, 'Okay, these people are crazy.'"

"We weren't supposed to meet," I said.

In 1995, my father wrote, "Empathize with your enemy."

That was the first lesson he took from Vietnam. In my life, I have also tried to practice empathy. But I don't want to have enemies. Not if I have any choice. In Danh's friendship, I felt myself evolving beyond the lessons of Robert McNamara.

In the summer of 2018, my son Sean traveled to Germany to visit Danh. Sean discovered that Danh is not just a visual artist but also an architect and craftsman of unusual talent and inspiration. They walked together through Goldenhoff, a small farm that Danh had created to explore land-based art expressions. Sean told me about the ancient barns that Danh had acquired, which he had retrofitted with planks of fourteen-inch-thick pine many meters long. Later, Sean spoke of Danh's deep understanding of wood and how to incorporate its texture, grain, and hue into complex building elements.

In the ensuing days, Sean told Danh the story of an old block of magnificent walnut trees, just a hundred yards from our farmhouse. This section of trees was destined to be removed, as their productivity had declined significantly over the years. That special place in the orchards, the home of giants, has great spiritual meaning to our family. I call it the Cathedral Block. We have celebrated thirty-four of our children's birthdays there as well as weddings, plus enjoying many long walks at sunrise and in the moonlight. In the Cathedral Block, we've rejoiced in harvests of plenty and have been patient when the crop was down. The thought of removing the grove had weighed heavily on me over the years. I delayed it time and time again by saying, "Oh just one more harvest. I'll wait until the yield declines a little more."

As Danh and Sean walked through the timbers of Danh's

barn in Germany, they came up with an idea for the Cathedral Block.

After the October harvest, we began to limb the trees at about twelve feet above the orchard floor. Our crews sawed the trunks at ground level, leaving fourteen-foot logs, some as wide as three feet at the base. Using excavators and forklifts, we stacked these logs in piles of fifty trunks all across the orchard.

We purchased a sawmill and milled the wood to different dimensions, textures, and shapes. Our goal was to then hire a portable sawyer to custom-mill the wood right in the orchard. Once the boards air-dried on the farm, which took about six months, Danh could use them. With the dark, flowing grain of the walnut boards and a team of carpenters, he could create works of art from the harvested timbers.

In the fall of 2019, Danh prepared for his first showing. He asked Sean to fill two forty-foot ocean containers with the wood that we milled on site. Sean loaded the containers with the rough-hewn walnut boards and several enormous, marvelous walnut stumps, and sent them to Germany. Sean then traveled to Berlin to spend the months of August and September working in Danh's woodshop. Together with Danh and his team of incredibly skilled woodworkers, they assembled the pieces that would be sent to London for the September 18, 2019, opening at the Marian Goodman Gallery of the exhibition titled Cathedral Block | Prayer Stage | Gun Stock.

Prayer Stage refers to the walnut bud. In April, when a walnut flower begins to open, its tiny leaves resemble two hands clasped in prayer. *Gun Stock* is the part of a rifle that holds the barrel of the gun and rests against the shoulder of the shooter. Black walnut wood has been used for centuries in gunstock.

The space Danh created was half exhibition—on the bottom floor—and half woodshop, on the top. Danh displayed a few art pieces and furniture designs from our black walnuts; the rest of the space was taken up by raw material. It was a new legacy for land that had once been an investment on the part of Robert McNamara; the fruits of that land were now turned toward the raw materials for a consecration of history, shared stories, and incalculable loss.

Danh has returned to our farm several times since we first met. Once, we were sitting together in the Cathedral Block, underneath one of the great giants. We had been talking at length about agriculture and politics—the need for change in California farming, the need for buy-in from leaders, the need for people to understand where their food comes from, and the cycles of the land. At a pause in this very long conversation, Danh looked to the sky and asked, "Is that a woodpecker?"

There was indeed a Red-headed Woodpecker placing nuts and other food in one of the Cathedral Block trees. Woodpeckers have this curious behavior; they create stores of supplies, like possessions.

At length, Danh got up and said, "Let's have a look at the border. It's truly a little bit more..."

"Comfortable?" I said.

We were speaking about the edge of the block, where that place of consecration and memory melts into the vibrant and living universe of the active orchards.

"You would call it comfortable?" he asked.

"Yes," I said. "Totally."

On the border of the Cathedral Block are several large walnut stumps to sit on. The border is where I've lived, that zone between the strongest love there is and the strongest anger. That's the space between waking into a glorious day and remembering the last thing from sleep, the face of a harrowing nightmare.

Danh and I walked there, continuing our conversation.

With Danh Vo in the Cathedral Block

EPILOGUE

When the movie *PT 109* came out, in June of 1963, Jackie Kennedy invited the entire Kennedy clan to watch it in the White House theater. Several members of the President's cabinet were also invited, along with their families. We, the McNamaras, were among the chosen ones.

I can remember this event as if it were yesterday. It was a warm summer evening in Washington. We made the drive to the White House, a route that was soon to be familiar to me. Sunlight was still streaming into the theater doors and the room was packed with kids as the film began. Jackie had set out large pillows for us to sit on. Children were running around everywhere. The President's rocking chair, draped in green fabric, was right up front for the best view.

The movie is based on JFK's service in the Navy during World War II. Cliff Robertson stars as John F. Kennedy. It was the first movie of its kind: a war thriller about a sitting US president. Once the lights went down and the movie flashed on the screen, I was mesmerized. The excitement of watching a war story set in the Pacific with the President in attendance was overwhelming to me as a thirteen-year-old. I wonder now what it is like to watch one's own exploits mythologized. I suppose Jack Kennedy had gotten used to it.

I strongly remember watching him watching himself. To me he seemed warm, exciting, and somewhat distant, even though the physical distance was short. I can't say that I knew him. But sitting on the floor so close to a man who was placed at the center of history, whose inauguration I had attended, how could I not fantasize about moving that impossible distance from his periphery to within his halo? From my pillow to the chair—a small step, great in the heart. My father was very close to the President, and this was something to be proud of.

I was in school at Sidwell Friends when President Kennedy was assassinated in Dallas. The news was spoken over the loudspeaker on that Friday afternoon. I don't remember our principal's exact words. We were told that school was closing and that our families were coming to school early to pick us up. The hallways were crowded but silent as the shock wave rolled us out the doors. Our first sock hop had been scheduled for that evening. I was president of the student council, and I had organized the dance. I had been looking forward to it, and it vanished in a flash. Saying this now, reflecting on myself as a middle schooler, I'm surprised to remember that I was a leader at that age. In my recent years in public service, I have found my footing in that role. I want to be in the know, I want to be remembered, and I want to be a change maker. Surely some of that desire comes from my close proximity to the President who was killed.

After the assassination, I spent a fair amount of time with Jackie Kennedy and her children. She moved into a home on N Street in Georgetown. I would visit Caroline and John after the end of my school day. They were much younger than me, and this was like a baby-sitting or big brother relationship. On occasion, I would bring John a model plane from my own collection. Together we would race up and down the staircase, pretending that we were flying, jumping from the last steps and flapping our arms in the air. I loved those times with the children. They helped me understand that life would go on. It distracted me from the pain of months and years following the assassination.

After the playdates, Jackie sent me several notes, writing on behalf of John, expressing his glee from our times together. In one of these, "he" says:

Dear Craig,

Thank you for my letter and my helicopter and my card of the mountain—I want to play with you if you come in my house. Craig, I have time to draw you a picture.

John then draws a "glider plane with no propeller," some "not very good planes," and a "dead swordfish bitten by a shark." I was old enough to appreciate that these were special notes, and I kept them.

It's unbelievable to me that I never again met John John. Although we were ten years apart in age, it would seem that our lives might have intersected. My father's relationship with Jackie grew stronger each year. But that's precisely the point: Dad rarely extended his personal life to me.

Reading John's cards today, I find them bittersweet—knowing of his early interest in planes, knowing how he died. More than that, they're haunting. That loss is like a strange and dissonant chord playing over memories of those times. It doesn't go away; it resounds. It reminds me of the feeling I have when remembering my short-lived relationship with Rich Rusk. We shared a singular experience of growing up in the foreign policy power structure, and of coming out of that experience with significant torments. But he's gone. Who else can share that with me?

Even the loss of a friend is incalculable and long-lasting. The unknown suffering, the silent wondering. When comparing that with the assassination of a President and the nightmare of a war, I am overwhelmed by the thought that nothing really goes away.

Some months ago, I was researching Jackie Kennedy's life after 1963. I found an article in *Vanity Fair*. The piece mentions my parents.

> When Secretary of Defense Bob McNamara and his wife, Marg, sent over two painted portraits of J.F.K. and urged her to accept one as a gift, Jackie realized that though she especially admired the smaller of the pair, which showed her late husband in a seated position, she simply could not bear to keep it. In anticipation of returning both paintings, she propped them up just outside her bedroom door. One evening in December,

young John emerged from Jackie's room. Spotting a portrait of his father, he removed a lollipop from his mouth and kissed the image, saying, "Good night, Daddy." Jackie related the episode to Marg McNamara by way of explanation as to why it would be impossible to have such a picture near. She said it brought to the surface too many things.

Rereading this article, sitting at my desk in my farm office, I find myself looking around at the many "portraits"—images, more accurately—of my father with which I have surrounded myself. On one wall I have a picture of him walking with LBJ. Close by, there is a picture of him in his old age, around the time of his interviews with Errol Morris. There's a picture of the two of us together on one of his birthdays, wearing coats and ties. There are disembodied portraits of him, like his silver calendar. On occasion I've polished the silver calendar, a process that has removed the oils left by my father's skin. Yet the calendar, to me, is the hand of my father. Whenever I lift it, I'm gripping my father's hand. It's a loving gesture.

Keeping an image nearby is painful. It's easier, in many ways, to throw that image away. Or, as Jackie contemplated, to refuse that image. Disowning my father, getting rid of his image, would enable the conviction that he is not part of me, that I am not like him, that his actions do not continue to weigh upon me, that they have faded from the lifeblood of the world and have run out on the reel of history. None of that would be true. To say that I hate him, to call him evil, to deny the love I have for him—these things would seem, temporarily, to relieve certain pressures. But they wouldn't be the truth. I don't want that, because I want to be honest. It's impossible not to be my father's son; I can't be but what I am. This is not the end for me.

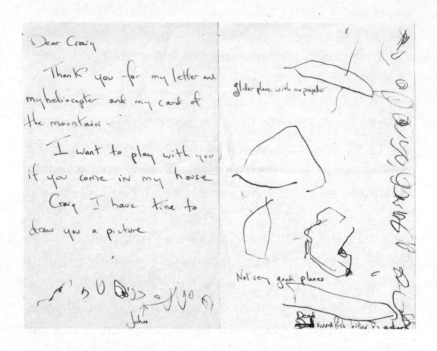

Jackie Kennedy's handwritten note to me on behalf of her son

ACKNOWLEDGMENTS

I've lived my life through the lens of the Vietnam War. My memoir is the story of this journey. It is the result of so much love and support from my family and friends, both new and old.

When my daughter and I traveled to Vietnam in 2017, we relied on the help of our stateside friends Lynn Novick, Nhu and Tom Miller, and Larry Berman, who introduced us to Thao Griffiths, Chuck Searcy, John Nguyen, Le Nuoi, and Vo Hong Nam. We felt the warm embrace of friends as we planned our trip, arrived in Hanoi, and lived the most recent chapters of this ongoing story.

Just as the war has determined how I have lived my life, my motorcycle trip to South America has remained my greatest source of inspiration. I could not have had two more trustworthy and adventurous *compañeros* than Will Rogers and Rob Deford.

To better understand my father and his role in history, I depended upon the most knowledgeable historians and storytellers. Daniel Ellsberg, Errol Morris, Phil Taubman, and Paul Hendrickson were invaluable. Together they shared many hours with me, helping me weave my thoughts into the fabric of the larger story.

While I was a fellow at the Stanford Distinguished Careers Institute (DCI), Sarah Frisch served as my mentor. I have been humbled and honored to have her as my coach during the two and a half years that it took me to write my memoir. Without her assistance in unpacking my story, it never would have been told. It was Sarah who introduced me to Jack Cubria, the writer who has been my partner in telling this story. Jack, I couldn't have done it without you.

I have the deepest appreciation for my DCI cohort. After dropping out of Stanford in the early '70s, I made up for my long academic hiatus in 2018 only because Phil Pizzo, founding director, believed in me. Stanford professors Alex Nemerov, Tom Ehrlich, Ed Porter, and Abraham Verghese deeply inspired me with their thought-provoking lectures.

When I began writing this manuscript, I had the same feeling that I had forty-five years ago as a beginning farmer. I depended on friends and fellow farmers for advice. As a beginning writer, I did the same. I asked Gary Hart, Michael Pollan, Steve Mayberg, Rayyane Tabet, and Adam Napolitan for their help. Fellow travelers Marcia Weese and Hilmar Blumberg inspired much of my writing about my trip to South America. When the time came to find an agent, my dear friends Jesse and Betsy Fink introduced me to Flip Brophy. Flip has been wonderful to work with, and to her I owe my introduction to Vanessa Mobley at Little, Brown.

Vanessa has become a trusted member of my family. Through Zoom, she has met my wife, Julie, our children, and our new family puppy. We bonded over our shared connections to Latin America and our belief in the importance of family. Vanessa is both kind and wise. She has been a constant source of ideas, and she brought a lot of joy to our work. She and her amazing team at Little, Brown championed me from the first day.

To my mother, father, and dear sisters, thank you for raising me, introducing me to nature, and loving me.

And to the love of my life, Julie, and our adult children, Graham, Sean, and Emily: I want you to know that your love has helped me reveal parts of my life that have never before been excavated. I am sharing with you my memoir in the hope that you will know me more fully, and that we may know each other more fully for the rest of our lives.

ABOUT THE AUTHOR

CRAIG MCNAMARA is an American businessman and farmer serving as the president and owner of Sierra Orchards, a walnut farm. McNamara is also the founder of the Center for Land-Based Learning. He was born in Ann Arbor, Michigan, and is the only son of US Secretary of Defense Robert McNamara.